Democracy, Bureaucracy, and Character

STUDIES IN GOVERNMENT
AND PUBLIC POLICY

Democracy, Bureaucracy, and Character
Founding Thought

William D. Richardson

University Press of Kansas

Published by the University Press of Kansas (Lawrence, Kansas 66049), which
was organized by the Kansas Board of Regents and is operated and funded by
Emporia State University, Fort Hays State University, Kansas State University,
Pittsburg State University, the University of Kansas, and Wichita State
University

Library of Congress Cataloging-in-Publication Data

Richardson, William D.
    Democracy, bureaucracy, and character : founding thought / William
D. Richardson.
        p.   cm.—(Studies in government and public policy)
    Includes bibliographical references and index.
    ISBN 0-7006-0824-9 —ISBN 0-7006-0825-7
    1. Administrative agencies—United States.   2. Bureaucracy—United
States.   3. Democracy—United States.   4. United States—
Constitutional history.   5. United States—Politics and government.
I. Title.   II. Series.
JK421.R513   1997
324.6'3'0973—dc21   96-51890

British Library Cataloguing in Publication Data is available.

Printed in the United States of America

10 9 8 7 6 5 4 3 2 1

The paper used in this publication meets the minimum requirements of the
American National Standard for Permanence of Paper for Printed Library
Materials Z39.48-1984.

To Robin, Gregory, Elizabeth,
and Kenneth

Contents

Preface

If the polls and pundits have gauged it correctly, America is immersed in a number of interrelated political debates about the proper form of its government, the policies that government should pursue, and the kinds of citizens the democratic republic should have. These issues are hardly simple ones amenable to a little procedural tinkering here or there. Whether we consider major shifts of power between the national and state governments, a move toward decentralization of power within governments, or specific public policies that seek to reform our taxes, modify our immigration, or transform our system of public education, the long-term consequences for the regime are potentially profound. Because these changes are almost always advanced under the banner of democracy, they have helped to rekindle the long debate about the proper limitations on government in our regime and, more particularly, about the appropriate role within it for such nondemocratic elements as public administration. This debate is entirely healthy for the world's oldest surviving democracy, not least because it has the potential to redirect attention to crucial portions of our Founding thought. In so doing, the present generation is invited to do what each of its predecessors has had to do to a greater or lesser extent, namely, to be reeducated in the explanations as to why the original constitutional arrangements were thought to be both suitable and justifiable for this particular people.

By using elements of Founding thought as a way of examining contemporary problems and issues of governance, in this particular book I seek to focus attention on the kinds of character traits the citizens were reliably expected to possess and the consequent effects such traits might be expected to have on their relationships with various governors. Obviously, one of the most troubled of such relationships at present concerns public administration. Because at all levels they are both the most numerous members of the government and the ones who, out of evident necessity, exercise fluctuating amounts of political discretion without clear lines of authority from the people themselves, public administrators have been characterized as "splendid hate" objects. What they do—and how they do it—is certainly limited by the character traits of the citizens. Of equal importance, though, is the effect administrative policies and behavior may have on those same traits.

Hence, in Chapter 1 I detail the interrelationship between the administrative state and the democratic citizenry it serves. The immediate focus in Chapter 2 is then on an appropriate understanding of the American character. Following this treatment, in Chapter 3 I look at the various ways in which our regime formally and informally provides correctives that complement that character in order to encourage appropriate public and private conduct. Next, in Chapter 4 I examine the role that reputation and honor play in shaping public virtues in America. Although the focus here will be principally on the conduct of public officials, the importance of those qualities for private conduct will also be explored. This approach logically then leads to a discussion in Chapter 5 of the education of the people who govern in America. In Chapter 6 I present a treatment of the relationship between public policies and American character, and in Chapter 7 I examine the consuming prevalence of ethics in American public administration from the perspective provided by Founding thought. I conclude in Chapter 8 with a look at the effects that some proposed reforms might have on both citizen character and public administration.

The genesis for this work began with a series of articles Lloyd G. Nigro and I wrote in the 1980s. Several sections of this book are built upon foundations that were first laid in our early work together, and I am grateful to the organizations that have granted me permission to use selections from their publications: "The Constitution and Administrative Ethics in America," *Administration and Society* 23 (November 1991): 275–87; "Administrative Ethics and Founding Thought: Constitutional Correctives, Honor, and Education," *Publication Administration Review* 47 (September/October 1987): 367–76; "Self-Interest Properly Understood: The American Character and Public Administration," *Administration and Society* 19 (August 1987): 157–77; and "Public Administration and the Foundations of the American Regime," in *The Revitalization of the Public Service,* ed. Robert Denhardt and Edward T. Jennings, Jr. (Columbia: Extension Publications, University of Missouri, 1987), 99–117.

Originally, Lloyd Nigro and I intended to write this book together, for it would have been the logical next step in our collaboration. Unfortunately, the demands of previous commitments, combined with a burdensome administrative position, compelled Lloyd to withdraw from the project. The book certainly would have benefited from his insight and wit. Instead, I am deeply grateful to Lloyd for the ways in which our early joint work provided a foundation for this book, but I must hasten to emphasize that the views expressed in it are mine and mine alone. Similarly, however comforting it might be to have companionship in these matters, any errors of omission or commission are attributable to no one but myself.

This book also would not have reached fruition without the confidence, support, and extraordinary patience that was unflaggingly shown by my editor, Mike Briggs. His assistance has thoroughly expanded my understanding of the difficulties associated with being an excellent editor. Without his informed tutelage I would never have known that there could be so many subtle and nuanced ways of encouraging, supporting, cajoling, and even goading an author to complete a manuscript.

Encouragement and suggestions were also supplied throughout this project by Phillip J. Cooper of the University of Vermont, a scholar and gentleman who has long been a cherished friend. Ralph C. Chandler of Western Michigan University and Lewis C. Mainzer of the University of Massachusetts, Amherst, reviewed an earlier version of the manuscript. Their suggestions certainly helped in the subsequent revisions, for which I thank them. Mrs. Thelma Williams also deserves special thanks for far more than the kind words and wonderful repasts she has so liberally dispensed in my department for nearly twenty years. Her example has always served as an effective reminder of all that is most honorable and decent about democratic citizenship and public service. I consider it a privilege to be numbered among her many friends.

Finally, it is somewhat traditional to express appreciation to loved ones for their support during the long process of nurturing a manuscript into being. In my case, the appreciation is deep and heartfelt. Without the tolerance, endurance, and patience of my wife, Robin, and the more sporadic indulgence of our two oldest children, Gregory and Elizabeth, this book would still be only a dimly remembered outline. And if their many sacrifices to assist the writing of the manuscript were not sufficient reason to bring closure to it, the prospective chaos that will accompany the impending arrival of a newborn certainly has provided more than enough incentive to do so.

1

Introduction

Bureaucracy . . . is despised and disparaged. It is attacked in the press,
popular magazines, and best sellers. It is denounced by the political
right and left. It is assaulted by molders of culture and professors of
academia. It is castigated by economists, sociologists, policy analysts,
political scientists, organization theorists, and social psychologists. It
is charged with a wide array of crimes, which we have grouped under
failure to perform; abuse of political power; and repression of employ-
ees, clients, and people in general. In short, bureaucracy stands as a
splendid hate object.

Charles Goodsell, The Case for Bureaucracy

The political message from the 1994 midterm elections, especially
as embodied in the Republicans' Contract with America, seems
clear: a large portion of the American citizenry wants a decrease
in the powers of the national government. The precise extent of the
desired reductions may be hazy and not well understood (by either
the citizenry or their elected representatives). Nevertheless, both
the rhetoric and the legislative activities of the Republican leaders
of Congress indicate that the principal focus of their efforts will be
directed toward the federal bureaucracy.

Under the circumstances, this focus should surprise absolutely no attentive student of the American political scene. After all, the underpinning logic of bureaucratic organization, and the hierarchical pattern of authority and power it requires, stands in rather stark contrast to the egalitarian, majoritarian, and highly individualistic ethos of the democratic regime. Intellectually and operationally, American public administration faces conflicting demands and constraints imposed by a regime that is at once heavily dependent on bureaucracy and deeply suspicious of it. Under the best of circumstances, the American bureaucrat has generally come to expect little more than grudging acceptance. (Indeed, at the depth of the Great Depression, a large percentage of Americans polled believed that cutting the public work force and trimming budgets could do nothing but help![1] Even Franklin Roosevelt, considered by many people the father of the American welfare state, ran a campaign against Hoover that promised a balanced budget, spending cuts, and reductions in federal personnel.)[2]

Bureaucratic capacity, power, and prestige are constrained, not eliminated, by the workings of the American regime. The constraint is not enough, however, to suit the critics who today denounce the administrative or welfare state. There is a revitalization movement taking place in the United States, but it is not urging a renewal of the public service or a strengthening of government's capabilities. Quite to the contrary, it urges the "restoration" of a set of horizontal means of social control and wealth creation-allocation, most notably voluntary democratic associations and the free competitive marketplace. Big government and public bureaucracy are accused of crippling these once vital institutions and, in the process, of depriving the American people of their independence and individualism. Like all revitalization movements, this one promises a great deal: renewed and unleashed, democracy, individual initiative, and the free market will allow America to restore liberty and to achieve unprecedented levels of security, wealth, and self-realization.[3]

Revitalization movements are not exercises in dispassionate analysis or the balanced evaluation of concepts and data. They are, rather, attacks on the status quo that attempt to convince us that we have lost or forgotten something spiritually or materially more valuable than what we have now. A necessary part of that process is discrediting existing arrangements or beliefs while putting forward a convincing case for an alternative that may be found in the near, or distant past. The resulting line of argumentation, therefore, is typically a more or less persuasive mix of creatively structured facts, outright fictions, often powerful myths and symbols, untested causal propositions, and non-negotiable assumptions.[4]

Unconvinced that the case against bureaucracy had been made, many students of American history, politics, economics, and government have had little difficulty finding gaping factual and logical holes to exploit before appreciative audiences.[5] A few illustrations are called for. Like Friedrich Hayek's true individualism, the free market is a theoretical construct, not an entity that America once had and then lost.[6] Jefferson's self-sufficient individualist was far more an ideal or image than a historical reality.[7] Unchecked, democracy carries with it the potential for a crushing majority tyranny, a type of regime that the Founders did everything possible to avoid.[8] For every instance of government regulation of market actors, at least ten examples of promotion and subsidization may be found. The American people, prone to condemn government programs and bureaucracy in general, are far more likely to be favorable when asked about specific services and agencies. Voluntary charity and welfare are notoriously unreliable and often inadequate responses to human suffering and disasters of all sorts.[9]

Much of the antibureaucratic rhetoric of the day, in other words, if taken literally, requires a suspension of disbelief, and some of the people who use it to mold and mobilize public opinion are fairly described as demagogic. Although it may offend rational sensibilities, demagogy is a common feature of mass democracies, and its use as a weapon against the welfare state and its supporters should come as no surprise. Max Weber, using the United States and the presidency as one of his examples, connected democracy, plebiscitary selection of leaders, and demagogy in no uncertain terms.

Active mass democratization means that the political leader is no longer proclaimed a candidate because he has proved himself in a circle of *honoratiores,* then becoming a leader because of his parliamentary accomplishments, but that he gains the trust and the faith of the masses in him and his power with the means of mass demagogy. In substance, this means a shift toward the *caesarist* mode of selection. Indeed every democracy tends in this direction. . . . Every kind of direct popular election of the supreme ruler and, beyond that, every kind of political power that rests on the confidence of the masses and not of parliament . . . lies on the road to . . . "pure" forms of caesarist acclamation. In particular, this is true of the President of the United States, whose superiority over parliament derives from his (formally) democratic nomination and election.[10]

Weber's observations apply equally to Franklin Roosevelt, who presided over a dramatic expansion of the federal government, and to Ronald Reagan, who is credited with initiating the current movement to achieve an equally impressive shrinking of "the bureaucracy."[11]

Thus it is important to recognize that any effort to revitalize the public service must inevitably be a political act, with all that such an attempt involves in a democracy. Absent a major crisis—economic or otherwise—the probability is very low that a political movement will arise (with effectively demagogic leaders) devoted to the expansion of an already considerable administrative and bureaucratic power in the society. Presently, the political current runs strongly in the opposite direction. This circumstance does not mean, however, that we should not make an effort to go beyond the rhetoric, to identify the basic elements of the contemporary challenge to the American administrative state and, then, critically to evaluate their validity.

Viewed from the perspective of history and political thought, a revitalization of the public service should be based on a fundamental assumption, namely, that any such revitalization ultimately will contribute to an overall strengthening of the American regime. Although enhancing bureaucratic capacity and building political support for the public service are important elements of revitalization, they must not occur at the expense of the institutions and ideals upon which the regime was established.[12] Therefore, my emphasis will be on revitalization understood as reform of existing institutions. The extremes of either vastly increased or drastically reduced bureaucratic power in American society thus are explicitly rejected.[13]

The reform orientation I offer throughout this book is not, however, uncritical; I will explore lines of criticism that focus on the character traits promoted by the Founders as being crucial for the development of the regime. In particular, I will concentrate on an influential critique that traces the challenge to the administrative state to its failure to preserve and promote the ideals of the Founders and the truths embodied in the economic and political concepts of traditional liberalism.

THE PERSISTENCE OF
THE ADMINISTRATIVE STATE

The term "administrative state" is commonly used to describe the great influence governmental agencies have on political, economic, and social relations within the modern nation.[14] The public sector of the mature administrative state is relatively large, is directly or indirectly involved in a broad range of social welfare and economic activities, and operates through bureaucratic organizations.[15] Applying these criteria, one sees that the United States unquestionably has constructed over the past sixty-plus years a firmly entrenched administrative state. It is an arrangement that is for all practical purposes indispensable to the American regime *as it is presently constituted.*[16]

Yet the arrangement is also controversial, and it is currently under severe attack from those individuals who believe that it has failed politically and economically while endangering basic American values and virtues. Candidates for public offices on all levels of government run against big government, and bureaucrats are portrayed as arrogant, greedy, incompetent, and abusers-of-power. Schools of business administration traditionally have prospered while enrollments in public administration programs continue to decline. Public administrators study "cutback management" strategies, and corporate leaders uncover systems that they consider to be massive inefficiencies in government programs, which may be remedied if private-sector management techniques are applied.[17] Economists and politicians extol the virtues of the free market, condemn regulation, and urge cuts in welfare and redistributive programs. Interest groups compete fiercely to protect what is "theirs" while lashing out at others who are "undeserving" beneficiaries.[18]

Through all of the controversy, the administrative state persists, and there is reason to believe that it will continue to play a major role in American society, primarily because a large majority of the American people would actually be reluctant to give up its many benefits—even while they excoriate the bureaucrats who deliver them.[19] An overview of the pattern of the U.S. economy over the past fifty years or so is instructive. For most of the years since the New Deal, the U.S. economy and other social indicators tracked steadily upward, leaving a society vastly more affluent and in many ways more secure than the one Franklin Roosevelt confronted in 1932.[20] Applying a variety of measures, the four decades beginning with FDR's first administration witnessed a steady expansion of the government's efforts to provide Social Security and insurance-related services. The numbers tell the story of a society attempting to realize Roosevelt's two "new freedoms": freedom from want and freedom from fear.[21] In 1958 prices, the per capita gross national product (GNP) rose from $1,154 in 1932 to $3,555 in 1970. At 46.8 in 1930, the per-man-hour Index of National Productivity had risen to 137.2 in 1970 (1958 = 100). In constant 1967 dollars, the median income of families and unrelated individuals increased from $4,013 in 1947 to $7,167 in 1970. Income distributions also changed dramatically: fully 65 percent of families and unattached individuals had incomes of $2,000 or less in 1929; by 1964 this figure had declined to 12 percent. Between 1932 and 1970, per capita disposable income rose from $921 to $2,610 (1958 prices).[22] In 1932 the public sector expended about 6.4 percent of the GNP on social welfare; in 1970 these expenditures were roughly 15.3 percent of the GNP. By 1970, 83.2 percent of the civilian labor force was covered by government social insurance programs, a large increase over the 52.2 percent covered in 1934. For the entire population, life expectancy increased from sixty in 1930 to seventy-one in 1970, and health care costs rose from $30 per capita in 1930 to $343 in 1970. And there are two other indicators of the social and economic changes that took place. In communication, by 1970, 90.5 percent of households had at least one telephone; in 1930, 35 percent were so equipped. In energy, 68 percent of all dwellings had electrical service in 1930, but only about 10 percent of farms had power; however, by 1956 these numbers had changed to 98 percent and 94 percent.[23] (It is also worth noting that much civil rights legislation—voting rights, housing, employment—was promulgated between 1964 and 1974, a period during which the powers of the federal bureaucracy expanded greatly.)[24] It is of course possible to question the extent to which some of these trends are directly attributable to specific government programs, but the fact remains that they have taken place within the framework of an expanding administrative state.

Although disputes over specific policies continued, and a large minority consistently expressed opposition to the steady expansion of government services and to the costs associated with them, between 1932 and 1965 public support for an active, welfare-oriented public sector was relatively strong across socioeconomic and demographic groupings. Opinionmakers, including politicians and intellectuals, were generally positive in their judgments concerning the administrative state that emerged during this period. Public employees (today's bureaucrats), though not accorded the prestige of business executives, doctors, or teachers, were seen as necessary.[25]

By most material standards the administrative state could not be counted a failure, and cases of blatant bureaucratic partisanship and corruption were unusual; but by 1965 public support had begun to erode. Of course, the reality of big and bureaucratic government did not change; indeed, by the mid-seventies, it was more central to the American way of life than it ever had been. Public expenditures on health, education, welfare, and regulation had risen rapidly. Programs proliferated as interest groups multiplied and became effective.[26] There was also a spreading perception that government was becoming too powerful and intrusive. Watergate and Vietnam deepened suspicion, cynicism, and outright hostility toward government. Public trust in and approval of government activities began a steep and rapid decline.[27]

Elected officials, sensing a major shift in public opinion, soon joined the growing chorus of those critics calling for less government, especially less federal government. At the same time, a relatively small and heretofore largely ignored group of academics and commentators began agitating for both general and specific reforms, many of which involved radical cuts in the scope and power of government on all levels.[28] It became commonplace to hear presidents, corporate executives, academics, and other influential individuals describe the behavior of bureaucrats in terms that made them appear somehow un-American, as subversive of the values underpinning the American regime.[29] In Goodsell's terms, bureaucracy was well on its way to becoming a hate object.

By the late 1970s, it was clear that the U.S. administrative state, and the approach to economic and social issues it embodied, was in political trouble. The elections of Jimmy Carter and Ronald Reagan served to emphasize a message that was becoming all too clear to observers of trends in public opinion—the concept of government and public administration as a necessary, positive social force, crafted and given political momentum during Roosevelt's first two terms, was being rejected by growing numbers of voters.[30]

For some of these observers, the reason for the decline of support for the administrative state may be found in its failure to bridge special interests and to sustain economic growth. John Kirlin, for example, concluded that "aggressive pluralism," as the dominant "policy paradigm" between 1965 and 1980, "encouraged an expansive public sector, the politicization of society along interest lines, and attempts to manage the economy through manipulation of demand and interest rates."[31] Kirlin saw the "disintegration" of aggressive pluralism as a result of economic stagnation, failures to achieve social policy objectives, and citizen disenchantment with interest-group politics. His description of the current state of affairs stresses political and economic performance: "Short of expanding fiscal resources, and with its claim to effective economic policy making and political legitimacy under severe challenge, aggressive pluralism lost [the] capacity to dominate policy formulation in this nation."[32] In short, in the eyes of many people, the administrative state has faltered because it could not sustain a supportive political coalition and because it failed to generate the wealth needed to maintain a steady improvement in the national standard of living. However, there is reason to believe the challenge to the administrative state also has causes that are much more profound than current attitudes and economic circumstances. Clearly, one of these causes is the uneasy relationship between bureaucracy and democracy within the American regime.

DEMOCRACY, BUREAUCRACY, AND THE AMERICAN REGIME

Woodrow Wilson believed that it should be possible to separate ingenious ways of sharpening knives from the motives of the assassins who developed these methods.[33] In the Wilsonian tradition, American public administration has been constantly preoccupied with the idea that "efficient" bureaucratic techniques and extensive administrative powers could be made congruent with, indeed supportive of, democratic institutions and virtues.[34] Having separated politics and administration, Wilson apparently believed that principles of an administrative science (some foreign, some domestic in origin) could be integrated with those of American democracy to yield a mutually reinforcing mix. Max Weber, however, saw this relationship in a substantially different light.

In effect, Weber argued that rational-legal bureaucracy and democracy are at once inextricably linked and antagonistic and therefore must be a constant and inescapable source of tension and conflict. Weber observed that democracy requires rational-legal bureaucracy instead of the administration by "notables" that takes place when the upper strata of a nondemocratic society also control the public administration. Democratic egalitarianism and universalism promote the development of highly impersonal, routinized, and professionalized administration that functions "without sympathy or enthusiasm," disinterested and unswayed by passions or causes.[35] Democracy requires bureaucracy as an alternative to "avocational administration by notables," but it inevitably turns on the cadre of professional, expert, impartial bureaucrats because they resist efforts to obtain "personalized treatment," insist on the consistent administration of the law in the face of majority as well as minority group passions, and exercise power as a product of their technical expertise and permanence.[36] In a description of what he saw to be a point of chronic friction between bureaucratic norms and the desires of the "masses," Weber anticipated a major source of social tension and political conflict in modern America.

> The propertyless masses especially are not served by the formal "equality before the law" and the "calculable" adjudication and administration demanded by bourgeois interests. Naturally, in their eyes justice and administration should serve to equalize their economic and social life-opportunities in the face of the propertied classes. Justice and administration can fulfill this function only if they assume a character that is informal. . . . Not only any sort of popular justice—which usually does not ask for reasons or norms—but also any intensive influence on the administration by so-called "public opinion"—that is, concerted action born of irrational "sentiments" and usually staged or directed by party bosses or the press—thwarts the rational course of justice.[37]

Herbert Kaufman, in an analysis of the reasons for the American public's "fear of bureaucracy," echoed Weber.

> A bureaucracy that scrupulously discharges its responsibilities *may for that very reason* appear arbitrary and high-handed to some observers. Conscientious attention to the entire body of relevant law thus makes public servants look like villains to some people.[38]

Kaufman also notes that the bureaucrat's tendency to resist rapid changes in policies and programs—often a result of the need to conform to existing laws and to solve the technical problems associated with designing new policies and procedures—frequently draws complaints that government is "unresponsive" to the shifting currents of public opinion.[39]

It would therefore probably come as no surprise to Weber that the highly rationalized and professionalized bureaucratic apparatus of the U.S. administrative state is constantly under fire from a public more than willing to call it incompetent, unresponsive, biased, and tyrannical; nor would he be especially shocked by contemporary attacks on bureaucracy by elected politicians and their followers. Wilson, on the other hand, would have reason to be disappointed in the results of almost a century of efforts to construct an American public administration congruent with democratic values and capable of efficiently carrying out the administrative tasks of the regime.

Changes in the American regime and the functions assigned to the state have also contributed greatly to public dissatisfaction with bureaucratic performance. Dwight Waldo, noting that the American regime, like all regimes, imposes limitations on administrative capacity, reminds us that the United States was established as a republic, not as a mass democracy:

> "Democracy" connoted to the Founders something little removed from mob rule. At that time the suffrage was restricted to approximately one adult male in twenty, but the Constitution,

even so, was constructed to prevent anything resembling quick and decisive majority rule. Even before the ink was dry on the Constitution, however, the tide of democracy began to flow. Nearly universal male suffrage was achieved by the 1860s and female suffrage by 1920. These changes plus many others, in institutions and in political beliefs, made the United States into a representative democracy in the course of less than a century and a half of evolution.[40]

Democratization, combined with nationalism, created conditions under which Americans saw themselves as "owners" of the government and, accordingly, as having a right at least to try to make it promote their interests.[41] And, to a considerable extent, the pursuit of self-interest in the democratic state has produced a large and complex governmental system attending to previously "private" problems and activities that have been made matters of "public" interest. As Waldo puts it, this socializing tendency

> has implications for the activities and functions of the government and thus of public administration. It advances us along a line marked by the nationalization of the monarchical state and the democratization of the nationalized state. It is a natural, though not necessarily inevitable, extension of the democratic state."[42]

Regarding the role or function of government under these regime changes, Waldo points out that public expectations have extended well beyond "core" and traditional "welfare" activities to include such goals as equality, individual dignity, and personal realization. Needless to say, these are demands that place enormous pressure on administrative organizations and, to the degree that expectations are not satisfied, frustrations increase and the most visible target for the resulting hostility is the public bureaucracy.[43]

Available administrative technologies, a republican form of government, continued expansion of what Alexis de Tocqueville called "equality of conditions," and the tensions produced by a rapidly changing national economy together impose severe limits on the degree to which American public administration is able to satisfy the demands placed upon it. Waldo aptly describes the situation of a public administration that must operate within a regime framework that often derails efforts to enhance capacity and efficiency:

There is this irony . . . that the activities and services a democracy increasingly seeks from government are made difficult to perform and to deliver by democratic restraints and expectations. Further, one can say that often public administration in a contemporary democracy is in fact directed to drift, and thus fated to fail.[44]

Another factor contributing to the unsettled relations between bureaucracy and democracy is the essentially elitist or hierarchical nature of the rationale constructed by administrative theorists to legitimate the power and authority of professional managers in both the public and private sectors. Administrative theory (some individuals would say ideology) establishes social and technical expertise as the basis of authority and power in modern organizations. William G. Scott, in a critical evaluation of the management philosophy of Chester Barnard, suggests that this value system runs counter to basic democratic precepts because it gives managers the "right" to inculcate motives, to educate, and to propagandize, in other words, to control behavior and to subordinate the individual to the collective.[45] Scott believes that this model of authority in organizations has been largely accepted, thus setting the stage for totalitarian politics. Frederick Thayer, in general agreement with Scott, argues that administrative/management concepts accepted by business and public administration are nothing more than a thinly veiled justification of hierarchy as an organizing principle in society.[46] Robert Denhardt attacks the idea that positive science and instrumentalism should provide the conceptual base of public administration, asserting that they do not allow democratic communication over basic purposes and values. Like Scott and Thayer, he sees a need to "democratize" organizations and the theories associated with them.[47] Otherwise, hierarchy and its legitimizing ideology will overwhelm democracy. Scott in particular is less than sanguine in his estimation of the current state of affairs:

> The immediate goal of value inculcation was to secure obedience to managerial authority, which suggested people's unquestioned acceptance of organizationally derived managerial values. The more distant aim was to extend the legitimation of managerial leadership across all institutions: public, private, and not-for-profit. The undoubted acquiescence by the majority of Americans to managerial governance for the last 35 years confirms the fulfillment of the Barnardian prophesy.[48]

Scott's conclusions would seem to confirm Friedrich Hayek's fear that centralized planning and authority would ultimately destroy what he believed to be the cornerstone of liberty: true individualism.[49] Written some forty years ago, Hayek's words are still relevant to the current debate over the administrative state's impact on democracy and individual self-sufficiency. He rejects the idea that anyone is in a position to know best: "Human Reason, with a capital R, does not exist in the singular, as given or available to any particular person, as the rationalist approach seems to presume, but must be conceived as an interpersonal process in which anyone's contribution is tested and corrected by others."[50]

More recently, for example, Charles Lindblom and Aaron Wildavsky have attempted to highlight the importance of the differences between bureaucratic rationalism and democratic interaction as ways of linking individual and social interests in the making and implementing of public policy.[51] After a century of efforts to build a professionalized public administration that is both "rational" and "responsive" to democratic processes, no truly integrative solution has emerged.[52] Hayek has described the issue:

> The real question, therefore, is not whether man is, or ought to be, guided by selfish motives but whether we can allow him

to be guided in his actions by those immediate consequences
which he can know and care for or whether he ought to be
made to do what seems appropriate to somebody else who is
supposed to possess a fuller comprehension of the significance of these actions to society as a whole.[53]

As the political rhetoric of the day amply demonstrates, this old
argument has lost little of its vitality. Consequently, although,
improved administrative performance (effectiveness-efficiency),
lowered levels of "win-lose" conflict among interest groups, sustained economic growth, and programs more in tune with majority preferences would probably raise aggregate levels of public
confidence in governmental institutions and reduce outright antipa-
thy toward the public service, there is reason to believe that bureaucracy will continue to be a problematic feature of the American
regime. More specifically, the nature of the relationship between
American democracy and its bureaucratic apparatus is characterized by tension, conflict, and competition. Each limits or resists the
other's tendencies toward expansion and domination; as vehicles
of honor, wealth, and power, they compete. Democracy assumes a
horizontal form of human association, stresses voluntarism, and
promotes individualism. Bureaucracy, on the other hand, is a vertical organization; it relies on technical expertise, exercises formal
authority and impartial rules, and is collectivist in orientation. Since
the republican arrangement deliberately incorporates and seeks to
balance both horizontal and vertical forms of governance and control, outright domination by either would fundamentally transform
the regime.[54]

Accordingly, in this book I will seek to bridge the admittedly
contradictory elements of American public administration and the
regime it is intended to serve by examining the complex interac-
tions of several elements. The binding thread that will run through
every discussion, though, will be a proper understanding of and
appreciation for the American character. Every type of regime, be
it democratic, aristocratic, or even tyrannical, fosters a certain type
of citizen or subject. For example, if it is to thrive and prosper, a

commercially oriented regime must more or less successfully inculcate among its citizenry such traits as rudimentary honesty, a desire for wealth, pacific habits (war consumes wealth), and some respectable degree of what we call the Protestant work ethic. Similarly, a militaristic regime desiring conquest must, above all else, produce good soldiers. Among other things, this generally means denigrating personal comfort (wealth), exalting honor, lauding the virtues of courage and patriotism, and encouraging aggressiveness. For public officials contemplating the introduction of a given policy, misperceiving (or, even worse, ignoring or disdaining) the fundamental orientation of one's citizenry can have disastrous consequences. With this in mind, I examine the peculiar American character that has such a decisive effect not only on the nature and kind of policies that can be introduced within the regime but also on the kind of governors who ultimately come to serve it.

2

Character, Administration, and the American Regime

[The American regime] has its foundations in the willing use of human passions and interests, but it has also certain enduring excellences necessary to its fulfillment. Preserving that foundation and, at the same time, nurturing the appropriate excellences is the task of enlightened American citizenship and statesmanship. It is easy to fail; easy to indulge a preference for liberty that exults only in the free play of the passions and interests and easy to make utopian demands for universal excellences which ignore the limiting requisites of the American political system.

Martin Diamond, "The American Idea of Man"

American public administrators play a major role in the governance of the regime because they routinely exercise broad discretionary powers. Toward the end of his essay on the study of administration, Woodrow Wilson asked a question concerning the character of the American public administrator that is as salient today as it was in 1887.

The question for us is, how shall our series of governments within governments be so administered that it shall always be to the interest of the public officer to serve, not his superior alone but the community also, with the best efforts of his talents and the soberest service of his conscience? How shall such service be made to his commonest interest by contributing abundantly to his sustenance, to his dearest interest by furthering his ambition, and to his highest interests by advancing his honor and establishing his character?[1]

Over the century that has passed since Wilson posed this question, students of American public administration have worked to provide answers. Government and civil service reform, professionalism, codes of ethics, legislative oversight, judicial review, and citizen participation have been put forward as ways to improve the chances that public administrators will consistently serve the public interest.[2] The explicit attention to the character of the public administrator called for by Wilson, however, has received far less attention than his desire for a "science" of administration.[3] At least in regard to the ethical content of public administration, Wilson framed the issue in a manner that placed it squarely in the Founding tradition. The very language he used reveals an attempt to link 1787 and 1887 and, in so doing, to connect clearly the science of administration with the ideas that form the foundations of the American regime.

Recognizing and encouraging the development of those virtues or excellences needed to sustain the American regime was unquestionably of concern to the men who established the nation. A close look at the thoughts of some participants in the Founding, therefore, offers at least a partial answer to the question posed by Wilson in the essay that is generally considered to have launched public administration as a self-conscious field of study.[4] Accordingly, I now focus on the potential contributions of Founding thought to current efforts to define and establish a public administration that is ethically excellent.

CITIZEN CHARACTER AND FOUNDING THOUGHT

The "black letter text" of the Constitution of the United States offers little if any explicit assistance to those seeking to understand the role of citizen character in the thinking of the Founders. Since Article 2 and related parts of the document do not go beyond general references to the powers, duties, and requirements of the executive branch, it is not surprising that there is equal vagueness regarding the character required of the individuals who would administer the affairs of the new national government.[5] The Constitution's silence on these matters, of course, is deceptive. The historical record, including the written works of the men who were delegates to the Constitutional Convention, reveals that their expectations, fears, and aspirations concerning citizen character were central to their deliberations over the powers and form of the new government.[6]

Although interpretations differ, students of American political thought agree on the point that the Constitution establishes a form of government designed to rest on qualities that the Founders understood to be the bedrock realities of human nature. Their views of human nature were largely derived from two sources: the careful study of ancient and modern political history and thought, and the clear failings of our first constitution, the Articles of Confederation. Because they really did not intend to establish any form of government other than a democracy (practically speaking, setting up a monarchy or aristocracy would have faced enormous political difficulties given the passionate opposition of substantial segments of the citizenry to the excesses of the British monarchy), the most immediate concerns of the Founders were with making democracy, so to speak, "safe for democrats."

The ancient onus attached to democracies is vividly explained by Aristotle, who made it the worst of his three forms of "wrong constitutions."[7] Democracy was burdened with this reputation because its fundamental principle of majority rule in reality meant "rule by the poorer classes" for their own advantage or interest. There was little reason to suppose that the interest of such a class was the same as (or even compatible with) the interest of the whole community. In short, such democracies tended to be hostile to minorities (such as the rich) that were not part of the ruling majority. It was not unknown for conflicts between these factions to produce passions of such a magnitude that civil wars ensued.

If democracies did not dissolve into ruinous civil war, there was always the prospect of superior foreign enemies (especially those from larger regimes ruled by monarchs or tyrants) overrunning the outnumbered democratic defenders. The reason for this vulnerability may also be found in what were then believed to be the inherent restrictions on the size of such regimes. Loosely following the spirit (if not the letter) of Aristotle's contention that the "good life" was the end humans sought to advance within political societies, democracies tended to be restricted in two interrelated ways: geographically they could not be so large that the citizens were precluded from conveniently coming together to decide the public's business, and numerically they were restrained by the view that, at a minimum, they had to be able to recognize their fellow citizens. The latter restriction was especially important, for it assumed that reputation (and, especially, "shame") would serve as a powerful constraint on the behavior of the citizenry.[8] The consequence of such views was that these small democracies normally had to form confederations for defense against external enemies.[9]

From our vantage point of nearly twenty-two decades of successful democratic rule, we might be excused for failing to appreciate the risks associated with the Founders' decision to establish a democratic form of government. Indeed, their very enthusiasm for such a government might be considered more than a little curious were it not for one important matter: their confident belief that they had come up with novel correctives to its most obvious shortcomings. In explaining their improvements, the Founders voiced a bold claim: modernity had made such considerable advancements in the "science of politics" that it could even be said that democracy had been "perfected."

If it had been found impracticable to have devised models of a more perfect structure [democracy would have had to be abandoned]. The science of politics, however, like most other sciences, has received great improvement. The efficacy of various principles is now well understood, which were either not known at all, or imperfectly known to the ancients. The regular distribution of power into distinct departments; the introduction of legislative balances and checks; the institution of courts composed of judges holding their offices during good behavior; the representation of the people in the legislature by deputies of their own election; *these are wholly new discoveries,* or have made their principal progress towards perfection in modern times.[10]

The status of these structural arrangements as "wholly new discoveries" was perhaps less important to the long-term success of the regime than was the particular understanding of human nature that gave rise to them. The Founders saw no reason to suppose that the citizenry of this (or any other) regime would be especially selfless or self-governing (in the ancient sense of that term). Since the governors were to be selected from among these self-same citizens, neither was there any expectation that they would be significantly more enlightened, knowledgeable, or virtuous than their fellows. Consequently, the Founders depended on the judicious channeling and clashing of certain features of human nature so as to better ensure that the good of the regime would ultimately benefit.

Since clashes between groups or classes of citizens historically had been a principal cause of the demise of democracies, attention was appropriately first directed to them. In the most famous of *The Federalist Papers,* Publius discusses how to control "factions" or, as we would today call them, interest groups. His solution was derived from the ancient understanding that man's nature was divisible into three parts. The smallest but most important of these was Reason (which ideally should rule over the others). Next in both order and relative size were the Passions, which (especially among democrats) were entirely capable of causing impulsive political behavior. Finally, the largest component of this division was reserved for the Desires, which, as the title implies, was the province of those driving forces concerned with satisfying the body and making its existence ever more comfortable.

Unfortunately, the proper arrangement of these three components so as to produce a self-governed individual was not at all a science (then or now). Nature had to assist by providing a suitably gifted human whose potential capacity to reason was considerable and whose passions and desires were unlikely to exercise gargantuan sway. Then the subtle influences of nurture—that is, education—had to be of just the right sort to maximize reason, channel the passions, and minimize the desires. In other words, the likelihood of consistently being able to produce many individuals ruled by reason in any regime (and above all in a democracy) was not seen as being particularly great.[11]

Not surprisingly, therefore, in the tenth essay of *The Federalist Papers* Publius assumes that man's reason will be "fallible" and that, as such, it alone would be a most uncertain foundation upon which to base a regime.[12] Yet he saw in this very fallibility one key to resolving that most intractable of democratic problems, namely, the obvious potential for the majority faction to have its way simply by tyrannizing over all other factions in the course of passionate domestic conflicts. As he put it, "As long as the reason of man continues fallible, and he is at liberty to exercise it, different opinions will be formed." If enough "different opinions" could be encouraged to flourish, it might be quite difficult for a majority opinion to form or, if formed, to hold together for very long. How, then, to provide such encouragement?

Since it might be more accurate to say that the mass of men can be relied upon to "mis-reason" more often than to reason correctly, Publius turned to that one part of human nature that all men assuredly possessed: the desires. Though traditionally viewed as the most base portion of human nature—one that might very well have to be controlled tyrannically through an alliance of reason and the passions—Publius instead saw a bedrock upon which to erect a certain kind of democratic regime.[13] Following the precepts of John Locke, he saw the unleashing of these base desires as having the potential for doing more good than harm to the regime. From a communal perspective, an individual's greed, properly channeled, could become the engine for the creation of more wealth for everyone.[14] (Embarking on this arrangement preordained that the regime would have citizens of a certain kind—more merchants than soldiers, more engineers than poets, more city dwellers than farmers, and so on.) Equally important—especially when considering the age-old problem of majority factions—the proper channeling of such unleashed desires could lead to a proliferation of minority opinions. If the desires are most concerned with bodily matters, and if their principal objective is not just preservation of the body but "comfortable self-preservation," the acquisition of all manner of "comfort-enhancing" kinds of property becomes of great importance.[15] Furthermore, if the prospect of augmenting or diminishing such property reliably could be expected to exert a powerful influence over the (already fallible) reasoning of most men most of the time, a base but sound corrective to the problem of cohesive majority opinion was at hand.

Arguing that the "the division of the society into different interests and parties" results from the influence property has "on the sentiments and views of the respective proprietors," Publius proposed to diversify property. Contending that the natural differences in "the faculties of men" is the original source of the "rights of property,"[16] Publius intended to establish a regime that enhanced rather than impeded these differences. Indeed, seeing these differences as "an insuperable obstacle to a uniformity of interests," Publius boldly proclaimed that the "protection of these [different] faculties is the *first object of government.*"[17] It is consequently from "the protection of different and unequal faculties of acquiring property . . . [that] the possession of different kinds and degrees of property immediately results."

In order to have the advantage of these "different kinds and degrees of property," a particular type of regime is required, namely, one that is unabashedly commercial. An agriculturally based regime has only limited opportunities to diversify its kinds of property. (It may do quite well in the different "degrees of property" category, though. There is ample historical evidence of agricultural regimes having vast disparities of wealth among their inhabitants.) How many different ways can one distinguish among the occupations of an agricultural community? How distinct are the property-influenced interests of a tiller, a sower, a harvester? (Or, for that matter, a farmer of corn as compared to one of wheat?) Only in a commercial regime with all its specialization is it possible to have such tremendous diversity in the ways of acquiring property that there is no single occupation capable of commanding a majority of the citizens.[18]

Viewed from the most base perspective, the citizens of this new democracy generally would be occupied with attempting to improve their material lot in life, which would mean that their principal efforts (and attention) would be focused on their own "kind" of property. Appropriately encouraged by the principles and structure of their regime, such individuals might be relied upon to become intensely passionate only if their particular kind of property became threatened.[19] By itself, such channeling of self-interest seemed to be an effective way of curtailing majority factions. But was it a sufficient foundation upon which to establish a democracy? The Founders thought not.

A second, critical component was added to bolster the defense against majoritarian factions: a regime would have to have a large land area over which to disperse the citizens. In direct opposition to the ancient notion that the extent of a democracy was limited in both geography and population by the ease with which the people could come together and know each other, the Founders made a virtue out of the extraordinary size of their regime. Spread out over the whole nation, members of any given minority faction would not only find it exceedingly difficult to come together to advance their interests, but they also would probably have great trouble even in identifying individuals who were just like themselves. The limitations of transportation and communication together would help to ensure that impassioned members of a faction would not easily be able to use their collective political power—at least not nationally and in person.[20]

The combination of a thriving commerce and a large land area indeed seemed to be a potent defense against the age-old problems of democracy. However, a citizenry that was encouraged to pursue its own private economic interests while spread far and wide throughout the land could not also be expected to be effective citizen-rulers when it came to public affairs. Hence, a third element was introduced to complete the eighteenth-century remedy for democracy's defects: the new regime was to be an "indirect democracy" or a republic. The citizens periodically would elect various representatives who were expected to serve more or less as filters of their constituents' views. Ideally, they were to fashion a more moderate public interest from the passionate and narrowly self-interested opinions of the electors.

One of the marvels of the Founders' tripartite plan for remedying the problems of democracy is the way in which each of the various components reinforces the others. Thus, the moderating role of the representatives actually becomes easier as both commerce and land area increases. The growth in factions based on additional "kinds and degrees" of property creates more and more minority groups (which are, in turn, spread throughout the land). The more numerous the factions contending for a representative's attention, the more likely it is that they will, in effect, cancel each other out (thereby making it possible for a representative who is so inclined to seek the moderate course).

The increase in factions even affects the type of representative who is elected. With numerous factions contending with each other within an election district, a potential representative must seek to fashion a majority (a winning coalition, if you will) in order to be elected. The most logical course is to appeal to those groups clustered around the moderate center and, to do that successfully, a candidate must adopt moderate positions.

In the discussion so far the importance of property has been stressed—all the imaginable kinds and degrees of it—in breaking up what historically have been the two most durable factions, the rich and the poor, into a multitude of small, self-interested, and politically "tamed" groups. The emphasis has been on the "desiring" aspect of human nature (and on impeding the ability to wield political power effectively or for very long on behalf of a passionate attachment to one's own bodily well-being). The Founders recognized, however, that formidable threats to the well-being of all regimes—and especially to democratic ones—were presented by the passionate attachments citizens might develop for certain political leaders or, even more ominously, for religions.

DEMOCRATIC LEADERSHIP AND CHARACTER

When contemporary Americans discuss their national political leaders, it is not surprising to hear them using such terms as "uninspiring," "average," even "mediocre." Far from being discouraged that such leaders are viewed, in a very real sense, as being "just like us," we should be celebrating their predominance. Indeed, the manner in which the constitutional structure divides us according to the "kind and degree" of property we possess also serves to cull those potential leaders who might be anything but average. The absence from the national stage of leaders who are, in Lincoln's marvelous phrase, "towering genius[es]" belonging to "the family of the lion, or the tribe of the eagle" has not come about by chance.[21] Napoleons or Caesars who would never be satisfied with "a gubernatorial or a presidential chair" never seem to make it to the national stage of our republic. Why? Is it not because the regime by and large has worked as intended and has successfully culled such individuals at the local or state level? (Or, at a minimum, has confined potential demagogues to those lower levels?) Such culling, of course, could also work to the regime's detriment, for it may be equally successful in blocking the truly exceptional individual who might have gone on to become our next Washington or Lincoln.

Clearly related, but less closely examined, are the implications of Founding thought on these matters for that group of citizens who would be public administrators.[22] *The Federalist Papers* provides perhaps the clearest evidence that public administration was of great concern to several of the Founders, most notably James Madison and Alexander Hamilton.[23] Publius argued that the federal executive should be energetic and competent and should govern in the public interest, and these attributes implicitly require that public administrators within that branch have certain appropriate character traits of their own.[24] Public administration also was expected to have an important role to play in cultivating citizen character. Rejecting the Anti-Federalists' argument for small and administratively weak governments, Hamilton asserted that a strong and competent public administration would command public support and "promote private and public morality by providing them with effective protection."[25]

There is, in short, ample reason to conclude that many of the most influential delegates to the Constitutional Convention thought that the character of public administrators was an important part of the foundation upon which they hoped the American regime would securely rest. They were not of one mind on this subject, but this is not surprising since they were also divided over the broader issue of citizen character and its relationship to political regimes.[26]

This conclusion is assuredly not the same, however, as asserting that American public administrators should have character traits superior to those of the ordinary citizen in order to play the role intended for them by the Founders. This particular line of reasoning has led at least one observer to cast the public administrator as one whose "primary responsibility [is] to end the isolation of the individual citizen from the essential character of citizenship."[27] More broadly, the question of the most appropriate ways in which public administrators may contribute to the development of citizenship has received considerable attention in the public administration literature.[28] A principal theme in these works is the idea that public administrators should assume a central role in guiding the citizenry toward a "proper" understanding of the public interest.[29] A number of commentators have gone even further, arguing that the public administrator should actively and directly promote a particular American character, one that supports certain "regime values."[30]

When one accepts the calling of the public service, it is presumed that one is committed to the American regime values. Since those values must be realized in the character of the individual, the honorable bureaucrat is automatically committed to the quest for moral nobility. . . . The Founders, admittedly, spent considerable time trying to design a system that would withstand the combined buffeting of Fate and weak character. But ultimately they believed that the success of the system would depend upon the virtue of its citizens and honor of its public servants. An essential characteristic of the honorable bureaucrat is a devotion to *noblesse oblige*—to moral nobility.[31]

Such an approach obviously imposes exceptionally difficult responsibilities on the American public administrator. Indeed, it requires the administrator to be a truly exceptional citizen, one more likely to be associated with a Platonic than a Lockean regime. For this individual, moral obligation is a fundamental part of public service:

> The "special relationship" that must exist between public servants and citizens in a democracy is founded upon the conscious knowledge about the citizens that they are loved by the bureaucracy. . . . The primary duty of public servants is to be the *guardians* and *guarantors* of the regime values for the American public.[32]

This is an extraordinary mandate, one with which the Founders certainly would have had considerable difficulty.[33] In their view, administrators, like the citizens and the individuals who govern, were not expected to be angels.[34] (To paraphrase Publius, if administrators were angels, neither external nor internal controls on them would be necessary.) This is not to say, however, that they did not believe exceptional individuals would be found in the regime. The Founders anticipated that there would be "ample opportunity for the emergence of a 'natural aristocracy,' " but the presence of such superior individuals could not be relied upon.[35] Therefore, they accepted as the bedrock of the regime that character trait most commonly in evidence, namely, acquisitive individualism.

In devising the constitutional framework the Founders worked from the premise that the American character would be self-interested to the point that the private sphere would normally be more important than the general welfare as a guide to individual behavior.

The individual usually would make the improvement of his own conditions the basis for political and economic choices. Therefore, the Founders argued for a republic on the grounds that acquisitive individualism was a predictable, if not an uplifting, trait whose negative features might better be controlled through a variety of restraints or "correctives" than by a reliance on the regime's capacity to reform the individual or on a faith in the perfectibility of man. Madison's point of view, which accepts the "modern" image of human nature as essentially self-interested, stressed the accommodation of these traits by the political institutions of the American regime:

> The interest of the man must be connected with the constitutional rights of the place. It may be a reflection on human nature, that such devices should be necessary to control the abuses of government. But what is government itself, but the greatest of all reflections on human nature? If men were angels, no government would be necessary. If angels were to govern men, neither external nor internal controls on government would be necessary.[36]

While allowing that there may be "few choice spirits" in government who might "act from more worthy motives," Alexander Hamilton expressed similar views about mankind in general. He contended that our most prevalent passions would ever be "ambition and interest," but he did not see them as a major impediment to the pursuit of the public good. Hamilton expected that a "wise" government would be able to make appropriate use of these passions in fashioning its public policies.[37]

Thus, in contrast to the classical concept of the *polis*, which saw the regime as a comprehensive system for the formation of character, the Founders relied on the tradition of Machiavelli, Hobbes, and Locke.[38] According to Martin Diamond,

> Because character formation was no longer the direct end of politics, the new science of politics could dispense with those

laws [by means of which the ancient philosophers had sought to improve human character] and, for the achievement of its lowered ends, could rely largely instead upon shrewd institutional arrangements of the powerful human passions and interests. Not to instruct and to transcend these passions and interests, but rather to channel them became the hallmark of modern politics. Politics could now concentrate upon the "realistic" task of directing man's passions and interests toward the achievement of those solid goods this earth has to offer: self-preservation and the protection of those individual liberties which are an integral part of that preservation and which make it decent and agreeable.[39]

Madison and Hamilton understood that acquisitive individualism was, by itself, an inadequate foundation for the regime they contemplated. Effective restraints were needed. They did not, however, choose to depend on a cadre of benevolent guardians; the correctives they established were given a constitutional basis. These shrewd arrangements were intended effectively to restrain both citizen and administrator, for one could not expect that the regime would always (or even usually) be governed by either enlightened aristocrats or exceptionally virtuous and benevolent administrators.[40] Thus, according to Herbert J. Storing,

This government is popular but not simply popular. It does not, however, rely on mystery or myth to check the fundamental popular impulse. "Nondemocratic" "elements" are at work . . . but they are out in the open. This government is like a glass-enclosed clock. Its "works" are visible to all and must be understood and accepted by all in order to function properly. Not many of the Framers were quite as confident as [James] Wilson of the reasonableness of the people, but the government they constructed was nevertheless understood by them all to be unusual in the relatively small demands it placed on a political aristocracy and in the relatively great demands it placed on the people.[41]

The Founders made a conscious and well-documented effort to minimize what they saw to be the undesirable effects of acquisitive individualism. The degree to which they succeeded is a continuing matter of controversy.[42]

There is, nonetheless, reason to believe that the Founders thought public administrators would have a meaningful role to play in maintaining the regime. The authors of *The Federalist Papers* clearly thought that effective administration was a key to popular support for and confidence in a federal government.[43] The Founders understood that public administration would serve the regime and the image of man that underpins it. In the optimum situation, the regime would be well served and maintained by fair, effective, and efficient administration.[44] Contained as well in the Founders' framework is a mandate to elected representatives, judges, and administrators: promote policies and administrative arrangements that take account of, are in accord with, and reinforce those attributes of human nature upon which the regime relies.

In the terms of such a mandate, American public administration does have a character-forming responsibility. Although this task requires an understanding of those character traits that form the moral foundation of the regime, it does not mean that public administrators must possess virtues superior to those of the citizens. As Martin Diamond points out, however, those excellences necessary to the regime must be recognized and nurtured.[45]

3

The Founders, Politics, and Administration

As an intellectual enterprise, American public administration admittedly has not made a very serious or sustained effort to build a foundation on the ideas and works of the individuals considered to be the Founders of the American regime.[1] Indeed, the few individual efforts that have been made are of fairly recent vintage.[2] The American version of the study of public administration is more typically presented as having its conceptual origins either in nineteenth-century German and French works or in Woodrow Wilson's famous essay (an effort that relied—however inaccurately—on these foreign sources). Although scholars generally do not draw undue attention to the fact that the intellectual and political foundations of these sources were firmly rooted in regimes with extensive aristocratic and monarchical traditions, the point is not inconsequential. In a circumstance wherein one is addressing the problems public administration has experienced in finding an appropriate foundation for itself within the thoroughgoing republican traditions of America, the issue of its early, nondemocratic intellectual influences deserves some mention.[3] As Herbert Storing observes, with the critical problem of slavery resolved by the Civil War, the great task of regime building and constitution making was finished. . . . The locus of the decisive problems of government had shifted from questions of constitution making and high politics to questions of administration. Wilson sought, then, to turn attention from largely obsolete and fruitless political controversy to the pressing and still unresolved problems of running the Constitution. . . . [He] proposed that the democracies look to the systematic administration that had taken place under *more autocratic governments,* with the view to developing and learning to use the science of administration, the fundamental premise of which is that there is *"but one rule of good administration for all governments alike."*[4]

Contemporary concerns with the relationship between public administration and good government recognize that the Founding fear of monarchical regimes is past. Indeed, from the vantage point of the end of the twentieth century, the American regime appears to have no truly formidable enemies on the world stage. Since the fall of the Berlin Wall, we have witnessed (what we may far too optimistically consider) the on-going triumph of the democratic form of government. Regimes throughout the world are making halting but discernible progress toward adopting variants of the American regime.

Of course, most serious treatments of public administration in the United States well recognize that our constitutional system has a major conditioning influence on institutional structures and processes. Similarly, it is not unusual to find references to the connections between the normal politics of the regime and the behaviors of bureaucrats and public policymakers. Understanding the American regime as a set of environmental constraints and contingencies, however, does not mean that Founding thought has had much of an influence on our ideas concerning the place or purpose of public administration in American politics and government. Nor, it seems, have we thought that the Founders had much to say to us about the standards to be used in judging the performances of public agencies and the actions of administrators. These conclusions at least are easily drawn from the relative lack of attention paid to Founding thought in the mainline public administration literature. This book is predicated on an entirely different point of view, one that seems to be amply supported by the available evidence, namely, that the Founders spoke clearly and forcefully about issues concerning the place of public administrators in the regime they contemplated. They offer important insights that may be applied to the contemporary debate over the proper sphere of public administration and the criteria that should be used to judge how good or bad our administration is.

THE FOUNDERS AND
PUBLIC ADMINISTRATION

Throughout this book, I consistently contend that *The Federalist Papers* provides perhaps the clearest evidence that public administration was of great concern to several of the Founders, most notably James Madison and Alexander Hamilton. Publius (the well-known nom de plume of Hamilton, Madison, and Jay) argued that the federal executive should be energetic and competent and should govern in the public interest and that these attributes implicitly require that public administrators within the executive branch also possess certain appropriate character traits.[5] Indeed, from this perspective, public administration also would have had an important role to play in cultivating citizen character. Rejecting the Anti-Federalists' argument for small and administratively weak governments, Publius asserted that a strong and competent public administration would command public support and "promote private and public morality by providing them with effective protection."[6]

There is reason to conclude that many of the most influential delegates to the Constitutional Convention believed that the character of public administrators was an important part of the foundation upon which they hoped the American regime would securely rest. Accordingly, there is considerable reason to disagree with individuals who would argue that the Founders and the ideas underpinning the Constitution they bequeathed to us are so out of date that they have little to contribute to the contemporary struggle to define and establish a truly excellent American public administration. Such an argument could not be further from the truth, especially with regard to questions centering on the governing functions of public administration in the American regime and on the character traits required of administrators who would carry out these functions.

Misreading the Founders in Contemporary Public Administration

With the Bicentennial of the Constitution, Founding thought began to get some much deserved attention in the stream of literature directed at students and practitioners of public administration. Among these studies, structural analyses—particularly those dealing with the separation of powers and representation—have been relatively popular. Some of these treatments have also served to direct attention to the fact that, over the past sixty years or so, the "administrative theories" of Jefferson and Hamilton have been receiving some scrutiny. The different approaches to administration of these two influential statesmen are generally set in the context of a long-running debate over the constitutional legitimacy of the federal administrative state. Frequently, the debate concerns the inherent tension within the American regime between the perceived need for administrative structures that are either *centralized* ones conducive to efficiency or *decentralized* ones that are comparatively inefficient but more protective of citizens' liberties.

Thomas Jefferson, after extensive travels in the monarchies of Great Britain and France, developed a firm distrust of a profligate "centralized bureaucratic control" that tends to govern "too much."[7] For him, the national government's proper sphere was foreign affairs; the administration of matters domestic was appropriately left to the states, whose smaller size would make them more attentive to the needs of the citizenry. As Lynton Caldwell notes, "He never could rid himself of the notion that centralization was a road to monarchy, and as late as 1823 he saw in the expansion of federal powers only the prelude to the institution of royal government."[8]

True to his agrarian, yeoman-citizen orientation, Jefferson also shared the citizenry's abiding distrust of public officials. (The similarities with today's political climate, wherein bureaucrats and politicians alike are, in Charles Goodsell's phrase, so regularly "despised and disparaged," is readily apparent.[9]) He firmly adhered to the Aristotelian notion of rotation in offices—and for him that meant all offices, elective and appointive. Service to one's regime was a duty that all men were expected to perform; the notion that one would seek to serve as a professional career would have been anathema to him.

Addressing the nation in the aftermath of the divisive election of 1800, Jefferson enunciated sixteen principles of "good government" that would serve to guide his administration.[10] In examining these and other related works, Caldwell emphasizes five "principles" of "wise administrative action": "harmony," "simplicity," provision for "change," "decentralization," and "responsibility."[11]

The patrician Jefferson feared centralized powers and, in various ways, sought to protect the liberties of the independent, democratic citizenry he so consistently championed, but Alexander Hamilton took an almost diametrically opposite perspective. Desiring political power to be the dominant domain of neither the few (rich) nor the many (poor), Hamilton diligently sought to expand the sources of potential influence in the new government. (His efforts in this regard are remarkably consistent with the tenets of *Federalist* No. 10.) Above all, he tirelessly and consistently sought to elevate the power and prestige of the federal government, believing that this was a prerequisite to the regime's future strength and prosperity. In the matter of administering important public policies, he thought the legislature's role was properly confined to that body's definition of its general goals and parameters. Beyond that, the executive branch (within which he saw public administration operating almost exclusively) should remain largely free of legislative interference in the course of its attempts to carry out those laws. He is also fondly remembered by some scholars for his understanding of public administration as an area that required comprehensive planning to link "the various aspects of public policy—finance, taxation, the regulation of commerce and industry, public works, education, agriculture, foreign policy, and national defense" appropriately into an interrelated whole.[12]

Much more recently, the relevance of Founding thought to matters of citizenship, citizen character, and administrative ethics has surfaced as an element of a more general concern for the standing of public administration within American society itself. With some notable exceptions, these writings generally employ aspects of Founding thought to support a particular point of view or prescription regarding administrative ethics and values. However, they do not present fully developed analyses of Founding precepts or their implications for contemporary issues and problems of public administration. This problem is particularly acute in matters relating to the Founders' ideas about human nature and its relationship to politics and governance in a democratic republic. Here the compulsion to revise (or to misread) seems almost irresistible.

Indeed, there appears to be some danger that the study of public administration is in the process of constructing a legitimating myth out of bits and pieces of Founding thought regarding citizen character in a republican form of government. This myth promotes a particularly distorted vision of the public administrator's necessary role in the governance of American society. It would not be the first time such a distortion has happened, as the case of Wilson's 1887 version of the politics/administration dichotomy and subsequent developments clearly illustrate.

Woodrow Wilson, it seems, set forth a politics/administration dichotomy that was based on a misreading of his German sources.[13] Wilson subsequently recognized his error, and his later writings effectively repudiated the dichotomy found in his 1887 essay. Those students thoroughly familiar with his work, therefore, are aware that it does not seek to establish a separation of politics and administration—quite the contrary. For the most part, early twentieth-century works on public administration by American authors did not even cite the essay, and students of the history of the field such as Paul Van Riper have challenged the idea that Wilson should be credited with launching the self-conscious study of public administration in the United States.[14] Nevertheless, the essay and the politics/administration dichotomy were embraced by later generations of public administrators who saw themselves as managers of a meritocracy that could best serve the public interest if it was effectively insulated from partisan and special-interest "politics."[15] In other words, the dichotomy and its famous author became key elements of a myth establishing the professional public manager as a central actor in the governance of the American regime and legitimating the shielding norm of neutral competence.

The important point, of course, is that the myth—rooted originally in Wilson's initial misreading and revived and nourished by those government and civil service reformers who had a distinctly political (if not partisan) interest in seeing it flourish—had very real effects on both the study and practice of public administration. By setting forth a concept of public administration that removed it from factional politics, the 1887 dichotomy reinforced those proponents who believed that governance of the regime was a matter far too important to be left to the politicians. Furthermore, it gave a cloak of legitimacy to efforts to shift a large part of that function to a nonelected "aristocracy of talent" or class of disinterested administrative generalists.

In the study of public administration, politics reemerged through the back doors of discretion and bureaucratic tactics, but these realities were addressed without raising two fundamental questions. What is the proper place for public administrators in the governance of the regime? What outlook and attributes of character are required of these individuals? Robert Miewald has observed that treating public administrators "as a special class in society not affected by ordinary human weaknesses produced a doctrine that effectively removed the bureaucrat from scholarly scrutiny."[16] One especially important consequence of assuming that public administrators are or can be "paragons of impartial wisdom" is to treat administration as a field of essentially structural questions, the objective being to implement arrangements that permit administrators to exercise their "enlightened knowledge."[17]

If public administration is treated as a form of politics, however, and the assumption is made that bureaucrats will not reliably be models of virtue, these questions cannot easily be avoided or treated as secondary issues.[18] Since the Founders subscribed to both points of view, their thoughts on these matters are potentially quite relevant.

The Founders' Perspective

If Publius is taken as the authority, the Founders did not think politics could be separated from government or administration. In *Federalist* No. 72, he writes, "The administration of government, in its largest sense, comprehends all the operations of the body politic, whether legislative, executive, or judiciary; but in its most usual and perhaps in its most precise signification, it is limited to executive details, and falls peculiarly within the province of the executive department."[19] In No. 72 and elsewhere in *The Federalist Papers,* Publius makes it quite clear that the purposes of republican government, factional politics, and the separation of powers make it impossible to remove executive details from the realm of administration in "its largest sense."[20]

There are no grounds for a politics/administration dichotomy in a Federalist system in which "all parts of the government became rulers and representatives of the people at the same time."[21] The representative, and therefore truly political, functions of public administrators under the Constitution were set forth by James Wilson and other Federalists who argued that "all government officials, including even the executive and judicial parts of the government, were agents of the people, not fundamentally different from the people's nominal representatives in the lower houses of the legislatures. . . . The different parts of the government were functionally but not substantially different."[22] Seen in this light, public administrators should not escape the general analyses of representation and of the character of representatives offered by the Federalists and the Anti-Federalists. Clearly, in the Federalist scheme, administration is best understood as a necessary form of politics intrinsic to the regime, and, in Jeremy Rabkin's words, "[Hamilton, Madison, and Jay] would probably have been astonished by the contemporary notion that the 'goodness or badness' of our 'administration' can be settled by impersonal, non-political standards."[23]

DISCRETION AND THE
EXERCISE OF POLITICAL POWER

If the politics/administrative dichotomy, in reality, has been little more than a "salutary myth" adopted for the useful political cover it provided,[24] it nevertheless points the way unerringly to a subject that deserves careful scrutiny. If this much discussed dichotomy was considered to be useful to administration in America, the obvious question is why. The answer starts with the unavoidable fact of administrative discretion and eventually leads straight to the fundamental issue of political legitimacy.

Whether one finds oneself in the position of administrator, governor, ruler, or manager, an insight into human nature sooner or later makes its way to the fore, namely, that human beings manifestly are different—indeed, unequal—in a bewildering number of ways. Never mind the all-too-well recognized visible distinctions of sex, age, race, beauty, or even size. There are more subtle (but politically important) ways in which humans differ—such as in their capacities and abilities to reason as well as in the extent and intensity of their passions. Such crucial matters as their willingness to assume greater or lesser risks and their motivations for a given action (be it a vote in favor of a school bond or a request for welfare benefits) frequently remain obscure, even to the most diligent of observers.

In the presence of such myriad differences, it is not difficult to understand why laws, regulations, and rules—if they truly aspire to channel and influence most of the behavior of most of their intended audiences most of the time—must by definition be general. If the net cast by such restraints is to encompass a large and diverse population, it must be broad enough to cover the dissimilar folk within it but not so finely crafted that exceptions cannot be made in the interest of justice.[25] (Thus the making of good laws, regulations, and rules might properly be considered an art rather than a science—especially if one has an expectation that such restraints will be voluntarily obeyed.)

The proper term for such exceptions-to-the-rule (or law or regulation) is *discretion,* and its use signifies that the individual who wields it has some degree of political power. For example, if a governor, manager, or administrator is able to facilitate or hinder a citizen's quest for some action or benefit by treating that individual differently from others seeking similar services, that person is exercising discretion.[26] Regardless of who is doing the facilitating or hindering, the end result is the same: citizens as a consequence are treated unequally. For all intents and purposes, the motivations behind the unequal treatment are immaterial. Yet we can with some confidence assume that such discretion is most often the result of good intentions. The wielder of it wants to assist someone who appears to be in greater need than someone else. As rational individuals, we generally take it as a given that administrators are basically decent human beings in a basically decent regime. Because they are also fallible, however, they sometimes err in their efforts. A consequence can be that they incite the passions of the very citizens they are seeking to benefit.[27]

In the not-so-distant past, when public administration was neither neutrally (nor otherwise) competent and lacked any pretension to being a profession, the exercise of such discretion was (both theoretically and politically) less of an issue. In its democratic heyday, public administration was a service performed by loyal partisans of a particular politician or party. There was no confusion: one acquired an administrative position because of demonstrated or promised loyalty and kept it by acceding to the patron's political wishes. One's claim to rule, so to speak, was clearly by proxy: the elected politician was the favored choice of that unquestionable democratic leviathan, the majority of the voters. Having won the votes of his constituents, the politician attempted to keep their favor by serving them in practical, tangible ways. The public administrator/servant was a principal instrument of that service and was expected to be diligent in nurturing the politician's relationship with the voters. When (and if) the politician failed at the polls, his successor was generally entitled to replace the loser's administrators with his own loyal partisans.[28] Whatever the well-documented demerits of this system, it had one fundamental strength: through it public administrators secured an impressive defense against criticisms about the appropriateness of permitting them to exercise the political power of discretion. Their claim to rule came to them in a direct line of descent from their politician-patron; dissatisfaction with an administrative outcome could be transmitted up that line to the higher authority who was clearly to be held accountable for the actions of his appointees.

THE QUEST FOR LEGITIMACY

However unsavory its operation may now seem to contemporary observers, the patronage basis of administering the citzenry's public business had an unimpeachable answer to the poignant question Herbert Storing posed about why one person should voluntarily obey another: "Who says?"[29] This two-word interrogative wonderfully captures the very essence of the problem of legitimacy. Why should I obey you (or any other person)? What, precisely, is the nature and source of the authority that makes you think I will comply?

Americans in particular have grown so accustomed to the effective working of majority rule that we generally act as if "consent of the governed" is the only source of "just" political power.[30] (The qualification is not insignificant; a fair portion of the contemporary political rhetoric about the extent and purpose of the bureaucracy's powers invokes this word in the course of an oftentimes passionate discussion of the proper place of administration in our regime.) Yet we seem to forget that, within the scope of recorded history, both the theory and the practice of acceding to the will of the majority is of comparatively modern vintage.[31] We could probably bear more frequent reminders that the establishment of our regime in its final form of 1787 was truly an experiment—one that could have failed.

Despite this concentration on democratic legitimacy,[32] the American regime acknowledges other sources, though it does not readily use them as a direct source of political power. Thus, in answer to the question posed by Jefferson (and later echoed by Tocqueville) about where in America is there a place for a natural aristocracy of talent, we might point with only slight hesitancy to sporting activities. Because they are tests of that which is visible—bodily prowess—and involve public contests that permit indisputable identification of the winners and losers, sporting events produce a large cadre of appropriate democratic heroes for us.[33] Frequently hailing from relatively humble origins, by dint of singular and extraordinary efforts these sports heroes take the gift of their natural physical advantages and go on to triumph. Because American citizens recognize both the athletes' achievements and the fact that they themselves cannot so compete, they seem easily to accept the athletic (and attendant social) prominence of the victors. (Occasionally such a hero is even able to translate the acclaim of the sporting life into political power by running for office.[34]) Because a particular athlete can so visibly answer a skeptical citizen's question—"Who says you are better than I am (at football, boxing, hurdles)?"—with actions that are undeniable proof of a superiority over the questioner, there is little ground for disputing the victor's receipt of a disproportionate share of those scarcities—wealth, fame, respect—valued by the American regime.

An alternative method of conferring legitimacy—one that this regime emphatically rejected at the time of its founding—is heredity. Once the dominant way of securing a claim to rule in nondemocratic regimes, its attractions are fairly obvious. There can be little overt dispute over the next successor to rule because the lineage of blood is more important than any other claim. Most commonly associated with aristocracies and monarchies, heredity may not produce the most fit successors, but it has one undeniable advantage: turmoil—including the prospect of civil war waged by disaffected aspirants to office—is dampened in the regime precisely because the heirs to power are known so long in advance. Still, with the exception of the political dynasties of certain families[35] and the role primogeniture once played in sustaining our aristocratically influenced southern plantations,[36] heredity has not been an acceptable way of establishing the legitimacy of one's claim to wield political power.

Historically, other attempts at establishing legitimacy have been based on such methods as force (understood as military prowess), divine right, and wisdom.[37] Whatever the relative merits of these respective approaches for establishing a claim to rule, they appear to be far less reliable today in sustaining or maintaining that rule. In consciously or unconsciously searching among the various traditional foundations of political legitimacy (majority election, natural superiority, heredity, force, divine right, and wisdom), American public administration has successively adopted several, sometimes in combination.

THE WAVERING LEGITIMACY
OF PUBLIC ADMINISTRATION

Once it rejected the one system—patronage—which was well grounded in the majoritarian approval that is democracy's principal source of legitmacy, public administration staked out an alternative that was as far removed from it as possible. Political neutrality—the contention that one is, for all intents and purposes, without any strong partisan beliefs and so is able to serve an elected official of one strongly held view as easily and as well as a successor harboring the opposite one—is a noticeably weak platform from which to launch a claim to wield political power. Taken to its logical extreme, it is the claim that one has no views about the important political questions of the time that one will confront on a daily basis (or, perhaps more realistically, none of sufficient consequence to be troubled about). If an administrator finds himself in a situation where there is a clear tension between personal views and public policies, the often-suggested resolution generally entailed an honorable resignation.[38]

Understandably, a posture of political neutrality has at least one powerful advantage when the partisan cannons are filling the air with invective: one is less likely to become a target. But public administration's adoption of political neutrality had another less practical rationale as well, for it was a sine qua non for the operation of modern science. Like political science, sociology, and business management, American public administration can trace its contemporary lineage straight back to the late nineteenth-century German influence on our own ideas of what, exactly, a "discipline" was and how institutions of higher education were supposed to teach and, hence, advance knowledge.[39] With a thinly veiled envy of the prestige accorded the natural sciences in their breathtaking pursuit of an understanding of the secret workings of nature, public administration (and, to varying degrees, the related social sciences) took a necessary step to bolster its claim to rule because of political neutrality: it contended that it also possessed a unique form of wisdom or expertise about government. As was emphatically the case with public administration's peers in biology, physics, and chemistry, the pursuit of truth (measured by the accumulation of replicable knowledge) required a scrupulous attentiveness to a rigorous methodology.[40] Political neutrality was an indisputable starting point for that process.

By presenting itself as possessing a body of knowledge concerned with expertise about government—and most especially about the more technical or structural aspects of governing, such as budgeting, organization, and personnel—public administration sought to legitimate its exercise of discretion by a claim of superior wisdom. The particular knowledge possessed by public administrators was not readily held by the ordinary citizen. Nevertheless, it was crucial to the smooth, efficient running of the governmental machinery of the modern American regime. Accordingly, these public administrators should be trusted to employ their specialized expertise in an impartial, just way because they were, after all, "politically neutral."[41]

Although in and of itself political neutrality was an insufficiently persuasive foundation for the discretion public administration necessarily had to be allowed in our democratic republic, it proved to be an impressive support for the claim of expertise. From this alliance it was but a short step to the establishment of professional associations and schools of public administration designed to nurture the accumulation of additional specialized knowledge.

This alliance served public administration as well as the nation reasonably well from the time of our great expansion of the federal government during FDR's tenure through its "second awakening" in LBJ's Great Society programs. However, by the time of the Nixon administration—especially the initial start of its ill-fated second term—there were strong indications that the citizenry's continued acceptance of at least the political neutrality basis of the alliance was coming into question. Not coincidentally, this period, stretching from the era of the divisive Vietnam conflict through to the present battles over abortion, school prayer, and family values, has been one in which great passions have rather consistently animated the citizenry. These passions, in turn, are being focused on our elected political leadership at all levels of government with the intent of stimulating changes—cultural, political, economic, and administrative.

If public administration is best suited for maintaining the regime (as opposed to an approach that may be required in times of "founding" or "revolutionary ferment"), perhaps it is really not so difficult to understand why it is the recipient of so much hostility today. If public administration functions best in a climate of Taylorian harmony where its technical expertise in structural areas such as budgeting, organization, and so forth can be best used, it indeed may be ill-suited to times that promise a series of major institutional, structural, social, and cultural changes. Although in the eyes of the citizenry the veneer of political neutrality may have all but slipped from the face of public administration, the context of the present debate is not wholly disadvantageous to its long-term vitality. When the issues turn (as they now are doing) to questions about the appropriate place within the regime for such anciently revered concepts as public virtue, honor, and reputation, both public administration and the nation may be beneficiaries. After all, the Founders had much to say about these matters, which periodically have been of continuing concern to many of the more influential friends of public administration.

4

Public Virtue, Honor, and Reputation

Is it, as one prominent commentator once contended, "chimerical" to seek a concern with "honor" and "public virtue" in a regime that is so clearly intent on pursuing wealth, comfort, and ease?[1] Is one almost equally misguided to seek these qualities among the governors of such a people—governors by and large drawn from the ranks of that same comfort-seeking citizenry? Although there is indeed tension—sometimes a great deal of tension—between our prevalent trait of "acquisitive individualism" and the demands imposed by pursuing honor and virtue, the importance of the latter for the soundness of the regime has consistently been recognized throughout our history. Indeed, as recently as 1989 we witnessed an interesting reaffirmation of this very recognition in the *Report of the President's Commission on Federal Ethics Law Reform,* for it was boldly titled *To Serve with Honor.*

> Ethical government means much more than laws. It is a spirit, an imbued code of conduct, an ethos. It is a climate in which, from the highest to the lowest ranks . . . some conduct is instinctively sensed as correct and other conduct as being beyond acceptance. . . . The futility of relying solely or principally on compulsion *to produce virtue* becomes even more

apparent when one considers that there is an obligation in a public official to be sure his actions appear ethical as well as be ethical. *The duty is to conduct one's office not only with honor but with perceived honor.*[2]

That the importance of honor and public virtue for the regime is still being trumpeted may somewhat overshadow the perception that the message seems to be heard a bit more than it is heeded. Thus, although *To Serve with Honor* may have offered the right words in its introduction, its charge specifically had to do with reforming laws. Promoting an understanding of the place of public virtue and honor within the regime was, admittedly, beyond its purpose. However, the issues that make honor and public virtue important today almost seem to demand such a context. Like so many large subjects, this one cannot be understood properly without starting at its beginning. For Americans, that means turning first to the Founding era.

PUBLIC VIRTUE AND
THE AMERICAN REGIME

A common theme that cuts across the well-documented disagreements among the men who were delegates to the Constitutional Convention is their conviction that the survival of the new regime would require some public virtue in individuals who governed. But how much? And could they reliably be expected to serve the public interest? Often their debates revolved around the questions of what constituted public virtue and how best to achieve it. Some participants contemplated a regime designed to produce an elevated form of public virtue involving "firmness, courage, endurance, industry, frugal living, strength, and above all, unremitting devotion to the weal of the public's corporate self, the community of virtuous men . . . [E]very man gave himself totally to the good of the public as a whole."[3] Others urged constitutional arrangements predicated on the assumption that public virtue of this sort would be a rare commodity. Since a democratic republic of some kind was contemplated, there was also disagreement over the extent to which its citizens would be able to identify and select virtuous governors. If ambitious, self-interested governors were to be the norm, what correctives were necessary to ensure that the consequences would not be fatal to the regime?

In one crucial area of dispute, that concerning which constitutional arrangement would be proposed for ratification by the states, the Federalists' position set forth in *The Federalist Papers* prevailed. The constitutional framework advocated by Publius accepted the premise that the American character would be self-interested to the point that the private sphere should normally be more important than the general welfare as a guide to action. In Publius's eyes, people were in the main ambitious and self-interested, and they should be expected to make the improvement of their own conditions the basis for political choices. Those who govern a free people, therefore, must seek to use and channel the motive of self-interest.[4] Alexander Hamilton bluntly made this point:

> Take mankind as they are, and what are they governed by? Their passions. There may be in every government a few choice spirits, who may act from more worthy motives. One great error is that we suppose mankind more honest than they are. *Our prevailing passions are ambition and interest;* and it will ever be the duty of a wise government to avail itself of these passions, in order to make them subservient to the public good; for these ever induce us to action.[5]

Led by Madison and Hamilton, the Federalists sought to establish a regime in which "choice spirits" need not be the norm. They were emphatically unwilling to write a constitution based on the assumption that virtuous governors would always be available and in office. Since these governors were to be drawn from the ranks of the governed, Publius argued that they could realistically be expected to resemble their fellow citizens in that they too would usually be self-interested. Thus, according to Martin Diamond, their objective was "a durable regime whose perpetuation require[d] nothing like the wisdom and virtue necessary for its creation."[6] Robert Horwitz uses even stronger language: "Pushing questions of virtue aside, they sought to develop political arrangements and institutions that would insure 'the existence and security of the government, *even in the absence of political virtue.*' ... The guiding and energizing principle of the community would be the vigorous pursuit of individual self-interest."[7] Diamond, however, goes on to ask: "But does not the intensity and kind of our modern problems seem to require of us a greater degree of reflection and public-spiritedness than the Founders thought sufficient for the men who came after them?"[8]

In fact, the Founders gave the phrase "public-spiritedness" a distinctly modern definition, one stressing the compatibility of self-interest, moderation, and service to the community.[9] Working from this perspective, the Founders reasoned that the American regime would be capable of producing a steady stream of people dedicated to public service.[10] Thus, as Publius explained,

> The aim of every political constitution is, or ought to be, first to obtain for rulers men who possess most wisdom to discern, and most virtue to pursue, the common good of the society; and, in the next place, to take the most effectual precautions for keeping them virtuous whilst they continue to hold their public trust.[11]

The writings of several delegates to the Constitutional Convention strongly indicate they shared the belief that those excellences of character needed to sustain the American regime would have their origins in one or more of three mutually reinforcing sources: constitutional correctives, a concern for reputation or honor, and an appropriate education. These writings substantially increase our understanding of how the Founders proposed to enhance the probability that Americans would be served by *publicly* virtuous governors.

CONSTITUTIONAL CORRECTIVES, PUBLIC VIRTUE, AND PUBLIC ADMINISTRATION

As a group, the Founders were painfully aware of the administrative failings of the Confederation, but they were divided over a series of questions relating to the jurisdiction and powers of the contemplated national government. All concerned recognized, at least in general terms, that these questions had serious administrative implications since the national government—whatever form it took—would have to be capable of fulfilling its domestic as well as its international responsibilities. Citizen character was a centerpiece of the debate, in part because of disagreement between those advocates of institutional arrangements that depended on high levels of public virtue in the citizenry and those delegates who believed, in John Adams's words, "that all projects of government, founded in the supposition or expectation of extraordinary degrees of virtue, are evidently chimerical."[12] There was, however, substantial agreement over the idea that constitutional arrangements should reflect certain assumptions about citizen character.

The Anti-Federalists argued that comparatively small, homogeneous, and highly democratic states offered the best opportunity to form citizen character around public virtues that would protect and nurture republican government.[13] In their view, the long-term survival of the Republic depended on the citizenry's adherence to community interests as opposed to individual or minority ones. They thought that a primary function of government should be the cultivation of public or civic virtue because "republican government depends on civic virtue, on a devotion to fellow citizens and to country so deeply instilled as to be almost as automatic and powerful as the natural devotion to self-interest."[14] In this respect the Anti-Federalists tended to mirror the classical conception of the regime as a comprehensive system for the formation of character in which the governors are to be judged by their commitment to the ethical purposes of the regime and their corresponding capacity to instill public virtue in the citizenry.[15]

Leaning heavily on the classical tradition, the Anti-Federalists opposed the extended commercial republic contemplated by the Federalists partly because they saw it as a threat to public virtue and, therefore, to a truly republican form of government.[16] They saw the small, homogeneous republic as a school of citizenship that carefully fostered the desirable habits and virtues among its members—a function that, if it survived at all in the large, heterogeneous, factionalized republic advocated by the Federalists, would not be fulfilled nearly as well.[17] If citizenship declined, they feared that popular control would be replaced by aristocratic rule. Accordingly, their arguments in opposition to ratification of the Constitution typically expressed such sentiments:

> It will be found that the form of government which holds those entrusted with power in the greatest responsibility to their constituents is best calculated for freemen. A republican, or free government can only exist where the body of the people are virtuous, and *where property is pretty equally divided.* In such a government the people are the sovereign and their sense or opinion is the criterion of every public measure; for when this ceases to be the case, the nature of the government is changed, and an aristocracy, monarchy or despotism will rise on its ruin.[18]

As expressed by Publius, the opposing Federalist point of view maintained that a constitution applying a "composition" of federal and national principles to an extended republic was necessary because people were not "angels" and, left to their own devices, could not select virtuous leaders with any consistent degree of accuracy. Publius's forceful criticism of republican approaches to public virtue—particularly their inability to homogenize the opinions, passions, and interests of a naturally diverse citizenry without destroying liberty—is well known. His treatment of the causes of factional politics and the corrective functions of an extended commercial republic still stands as the clearest, most powerful statement of this perspective on the connections between citizen character and the American regime.[19] In this view, the belief that democratic citizens and governors would possess superior virtues simply could not be relied upon as the foundation of the regime. Accordingly, the alternative was to accept as the bedrock of the regime that low-level trait most commonly in evidence, namely, self-interest.

Further, Publius applied this point of view to the "interior structure of the government" in order to see to it that ambition counteracted ambition and that the "interest of the man [was] connected to the constitutional rights of the place."[20] In this context, Robert Goldwin observes that ambition and self-interest are so fundamental to Publius's design that "if officials in one part of the government should be insufficiently moved by ambition and self-interest, a necessary balancing restraint would be lacking. . . . As fundamental as separation of powers is as a principle in the Constitution, that office holders must be ambitious and self-interested is even more fundamental."[21]

The larger argument between the Federalists and Anti-Federalists over the proper constitutional approach to citizen character was resolved largely in favor of the Federalists' position. For advocates such as Madison and Hamilton, effectively to channel human passions and interests was the most important goal. Yet the Federalists recognized that, by itself, self-interest was certainly an inadequate foundation for the regime they contemplated. Restraints were assuredly needed. They emphatically did not, however, choose to rely on the availability of an aristocracy of virtuous governors to achieve that restraint: citizens, elected governors, and administrators were to be restrained by *constitutional correctives.*

Particularly with respect to the crucial "discretionary" political power wielded by public administrators, this system of correctives necessarily requires that administrators both appreciate and actively support the regime. This view has led John Rohr, for example, to argue that ethical standards "derived" from regime values should apply to administrators because they are sworn to defend that regime. In this context, he points out that Supreme Court procedures and opinions often "teach" enduring principles, offer insightful interpretations of American values, have direct applicability to administrative actions, and raise questions "that are useful for reflection on fundamental values."[22]

Another constitutional corrective, the extended commercial republic with its multiplicity of interests (which Publius called "a republican remedy for the diseases most incident to republican government") is similarly seen by Stephen Bailey as a source of administrative obligation.

A large part of the art of public service is in the capacity to harness private and personal interests to public interest causes. Those who will not traffic in personal and private interests (if such interests are themselves within the law) to the point of engaging their support on behalf of causes in which both public and private interests are served, are, in terms of moral temper, unfit for public responsibility.[23]

While recognizing the need for governors (both elected ones as well as public administrators) to have a proper appreciation of the forces at work in their regime, the great difficulty has always been in how to harness the private interest most effectively so that it works in tandem with the larger interests of the community as a whole.

HONOR, REPUTATION, AND PUBLIC VIRTUES

Although the Founders sought ways in which the interests and passions of the people who govern could be channeled so as to result in publicly virtuous behavior, they also thought it only prudent to assume that the most reliable of these qualities would be self-interest and ambition. Nevertheless, in Forrest McDonald's words, they

expected something better, for men are driven by a variety of passions, and many of these—love of fame, of glory, of country, for example, are noble. When any such passion becomes a man's ruling passion, he must necessarily live his life in virtuous service to the public; and it was such men whom the nationalists counted on to govern others through their baser passions.[24]

In the case of the statesmanlike governor, self-interest, molded by a higher passion, becomes the vehicle that ultimately produces the required public virtue.[25]

McDonald, employing the example of George Washington, suggests that the Federalists subscribed to the idea that "public persons are and should be governed mainly 'by the law of *honour or outward esteem.*' "[26] A desire for the esteem of people of high reputation should be the guiding standard of individuals in public life: "To others be true, seek the esteem of the wise and the virtuous, and it follows that thou cannot then be false to thyself—or to the republic."[27]

The love of honor, however, is no easy standard to develop or, even more important, to use as a guide for one's life. For the purposes of discussing honor in the context of Founding thought, it is helpful to concentrate on three of its more problematic aspects: seeking honor may well mean that one values being lauded for possessing a given virtue more than *the virtue* itself; there are *types of honor* that may not be appropriate for a republic; and it is important *from whom one seeks honor.*

In one of the more important treatments of the subject, Aristotle discusses the differences between, in effect, being honored and being honorable.[28] In the former case, one seeks approbation for a virtue or virtues one may well not even possess. (Indeed, if one wants the public esteem badly enough, one may even act in opposition to the virtue for which one is honored. Thus, an ambitious politician who is routinely honored for honesty may readily lie, cheat, and steal in order to retain the office that gives him such public visibility.) The saving factor here, though, is that it is possible to acquire the desired virtues through habituation; that is, as a result of acting as if one has them, one may eventually come to possess them.[29]

Though not an exact distinction, there also is a relation between *type* of regime and honors. As Lorraine and Thomas Pangle point out, it is a critical matter whether one is seeking "monarchical" or "republican" honor.[30] The former tends to be class based—by means of its (often exaggerated) mannerisms of politeness and a concept of honor centered on peers, the aristocracy decisively displays its disdain for the underclass—but the latter, in its highest form, most appropriately displays a respect for that which is most to be valued in a republic, namely, the law. Thus George Washington serves as an ideal exemplar, for he carefully nourished the long-term needs of his regime (and clearly subordinated his own love of fame to them since his existing reputation for greatness would have been sorely jeopardized by the likely prospects of failure in several cases that he championed). For instance, he answered the summons to lead the Continental Army, served as the nation's first president, and established its tradition of no more than two terms. By his words and, more important, his actions, he served as a visible role model to all subsequent officeholders of America. His legacy was one of moderation, probity, and a carefully tempered love of republican honors.

Finally, from whom one seeks honor and approbation is almost as important as for what one is honored. Insofar as it concerns republican regimes, the classical perspective held that one earned the honors of a temperate citizenry by attending to that which was good for them (which was not always the same as what they themselves might have thought was good). The respect and admiration of such yeoman citizens, however, was considerably different in kind from that rendered by factions of their intemperate brethren. In other words, it is entirely possible for a republican governor to be honored for words and actions that dishonor republican principles—especially the all-important one of respect for the law. Therefore, it is appropriate to consider the source of honors in evaluating their importance and worth. Hence, in a republic, honors bestowed by one's peers (or superiors) may well be of considerable significance—most especially so if those peers themselves possess the essential virtues valued by the regime.

The importance of tendering appropriate honors was advanced in other ways that are significant for this inquiry. For example, it is found in the influential works of Adam Smith, particularly in his *Theory of Moral Sentiments:* "Man naturally desires, not only to be loved, but to be lovely; or to be that thing which is the natural and proper object of love. He naturally dreads, not only to be hated, but to be hateful."[31] Smith, however, assigned priority to the love of "praise-worthiness." Indeed, his interpretation of the relationship between self-approbation and the approbation of others seems particularly relevant to the situation of the contemporary American public administrator.

> The love and admiration which we naturally conceive for those whose character and conduct we approve of, necessarily dispose us to desire to become ourselves the objects of the like agreeable sentiments. . . . Neither can we be satisfied with being merely admired for what other people are admired. We must at least believe ourselves to be admirable for what they are admirable. . . . But it greatly confirms this happiness and contentment when we find that other people . . . see them precisely in the same light in which we ourselves had seen them. Their approbation necessarily confirms our own self-approbation. Their approbation necessarily confirms our own sense of our own praise-worthiness.[32]

John Locke, who was widely read in the American colonies, similarly emphasized the individual's concern with reputation and its social uses. He argued that the "law of public opinion" was a powerful (indeed socially necessary) element in controlling behavior. He reasoned that the law of public opinion is so effective because people have a strong need to be held in high esteem and greatly fear public shame or disgrace.[33]

Not surprisingly, the Founders understood the significance of advancing the connection between the honor of public servants and their service to the community. Accordingly, they sought to use what they saw to be a basic human concern for reputation and love of praiseworthiness. Their constitutional design is one intended to channel these private passions into those public excellences appropriate to (and needed by) the American regime. However, if this channeling is in fact fundamental to the regime's capacity to produce publicly virtuous or excellent public administrators, how can it be achieved in a regime that is now considerably more democratic than that contemplated by most of the Founders?

HONOR AND CONTEMPORARY PUBLIC ADMINISTRATION

With regard to reputation, it has been a long time since civil servants have been held in high esteem by the general citizenry. Recently, public scorn, often fueled by the words and actions of elected officials, has reached the point where some individuals in the community of public administrators have seen the need to publish polemical defenses of bureaucracy.[34] Efforts also have been made to provide (or at least to revive) constitutionally grounded justifications of the "administrative state."[35] Other writers have been content to warn of an erosion of morale and of competence as government loses (as well as fails to attract) qualified personnel.[36] Yet none of the criticism is unique. Complaints about tyrannical, incompetent, and self-interested officials date from the colonial period, and the constitutional framework provides no explicit legitimation of bureaucratic power, however real that power may be. In short, in the United States, the public service has never been an easy road to honor and high levels of public approbation.

To whom do contemporary public administrators look for approbation and, hence, whom do they seek to emulate? Clearly, the Founders intended that, within limits, "public opinion" would be heard and heeded in a democratic republic. As Herbert Storing points out, they saw no need for an administrative aristocracy operating according to its own idea of the public interest and independent of the formative influence of majority public opinion. If they were correct in believing that public virtue is closely connected to reputation and approbation, must it necessarily suffer when those people who want to be praised and to see themselves as praiseworthy are not reinforced by public approval?

In "The Study of Administration," Woodrow Wilson recognized this issue. In the course of his argument for a highly professionalized corps of civil servants having extensive discretion, he asked,

> To whom is official trustworthiness to be disclosed, and by who[m] is it to be rewarded? Is the official to look to the public for his meed of praise and his push of promotion, or only to his superior in office? Are the people to be called in to settle administrative discipline as they are called in to settle constitutional principles? These questions evidently find their root in what is undoubtedly the fundamental problem of this whole study. That problem is: What part shall public opinion take in the conduct of administration?[37]

Wilson's answer placed the public in the role of "superintending" the legislative and executive policymaking processes while leaving the day-to-day public administration in the hands of specially schooled and efficiently organized civil servants. In reply to those critics who might complain that he was advocating the creation of an "offensive official class," Wilson stated that "administration in the United States must be at all points sensitive to public opinion" and earn its praise through "hearty allegiance to the policy of the government."[38] Since the American regime rests solidly on the principle of majority rule, Wilson understood that any fundamental solution to the problem of public approbation would have to be grounded in that majority's opinion. His solution included a call for civil service reform and professionalism: "If we are to improve public opinion, which is the motive power of government, we must prepare better officials as the *apparatus* of government."[39]

Although the public service since Wilson's time has clearly improved in the sense of being a technically trained, merit-based part of the government, such progress has not resulted in any comparable improvement in the way the majority of the citizenry seems to view it. Under these circumstances, the Founding strategy would appear to stand a better chance of success if the range of those people to whom public administrators look for approval were severely narrowed. Along these lines, a favored approach in the United States has been to attempt to build a foundation for public virtue through professionalization and codes of ethics for public administrators. The public service is now highly professionalized (staffed by a wide variety of experts), but most students of the field believe that public administration itself has not achieved the status of a recognized profession. The desirability of such a profession, of course, has been the subject of lively debate since Wilson's essay.[40] Despite these difficulties, many academics and practitioners have urged that professional standards be adopted and applied uniformly to all administrators.[41] In part, the aim is to provide a reference group of professional peers to guide and evaluate behavior. The possibility remains unresolved that substantial differences between public opinion and professional norms could arise—even to the point that what Wilson called the "offensive administrative class" could emerge.

Stephen Bailey and Frederick Mosher are perhaps the best-known commentators on the tensions between professional standards and democratic norms.[42] Both men accept the inevitability of a government dominated by professionals who exert significant influence on public policies. The problem may be that these same individuals see little or no *honor* in such service to democratic norms or constitutional principles. If professional peers are to be the primary points of reference for public administrators, education may be the most effective way of orienting them to these standards.

> For better or worse—or better *and* worse—much of our government is now in the hands of professionals (including scientists). The choice of these professionals, the determination of their skills, and the content of their work are now principally determined, not by general governmental agencies, but by their own professional elites, professional organizations, and the institutions and faculties of higher education. . . . The

need for broadening, for humanizing, and in some fields, for lengthening professional education programs may in the long run prove more crucial to governmental response to societal problems than any amount of civil service reform.[43]

NURTURING "CERTAIN ENDURING EXCELLENCES"

The Founders probably would not have disapproved of the post-Wilson preoccupation with public administration as an instrumental field. But they also are likely to have considered it to be incomplete because it neglected the development of desirable public virtues. The contemporary interest in ethics for public administrators in reality is consistent with the Founders' view that, left to itself, the citizenry (of whom public administrators are a part) would act in a self-interested manner. The problem, however, is that the regime requires public administrators who reliably will be expected to act in the public's behalf.[44]

The Founders understood that the new nation required "certain enduring excellences." Although there is no reason to believe that the Founders anticipated the size, scope, and complexity of today's administrative state, they did anticipate that the quality of public administration under the Constitution would play a major role in determining the success of their experiment in a democratic-republican form of government. "Nurturing the appropriate excellences," therefore, is a challenge of particular importance to American public administration.

This reading of Founding intentions reveals a heavy reliance on the *interaction* of constitutional correctives with such matters as honor, reputation, and education in order to produce virtuous public officials who would serve the regime "with the best efforts of [their] talents and the soberest service of [their] conscience." Seen in this light, Woodrow Wilson's often-quoted assertion that "it is getting harder to *run* a constitution than to frame one" becomes far more than a call for rational organization and efficiency. It is also a reaffirmation of the Founders' belief that the promise of the American regime could be fulfilled only if the individuals who govern are committed to preserving and strengthening the foundations upon which it rests. This is the issue that Wilson recognized and that, more recently, other students of American public administration have raised in a variety of contexts.[45]

Public administrators should understand the importance and function of constitutional correctives. As Wilson recognized, their education clearly must encompass far more than a simple description of the Constitution. The public administrator will be well served by a thorough grounding in American political thought and constitutional history and law.[46] Public administration is an imprecisely defined field, open to many prescriptions regarding the preparation of its practitioners; however, in the American setting, no definition could sensibly exclude these topics and an examination of their applications to the administrative enterprise.

The study of the Constitution and the ideas that underpin it should provide a major element of public administrators' understanding of the duties and obligations that flow from a commitment to the regime. Yet as Wilson wrote, particular attention must be paid to the problem of how best to integrate the *self-interest* of the public administrator with service to the community or public interest. (With the possible exception of Jefferson, the Founders had little confidence in noblesse oblige as the moral foundation of the Republic.)

Concern for reputation—the desire for approbation or honor—is fundamental to the Founders' design. For the people who govern, to be well educated meant a proper orientation to the "law of public opinion" or to the standards and judgments of the individuals we are taught to admire. In contemporary terminology, public virtue is the result of orienting oneself to a reference group that values service to the regime, community, and other people. On the one hand, it is to this group that the individual looks for guidance and approbation. On the other, it is their disapproval that is most feared and, therefore, to be avoided.

Is it then unethical somehow to want to be honored by the public, to seek the esteem of one's peers? Clearly not. But . . . the relevant distinction is between doing right, helping people who need help, preserving democratic government, achieving some measure of excellence, on the one hand, and being honored for its own sake, on the other. In the end, then, the desire for honor, which is inherently selfish, can be redeemed only by seeking to satisfy it through service to others.[47]

The greatest irony of public administration since Wilson's essay of 1887 may lie in the success of policies and practices designed to avoid the creation of any system resembling an American administrative class. In combination with the emphasis on technical expertise or public management, the lack of any identifiable community of public administrators may have seriously eroded the foundations upon which the Founders relied to ensure that the regime would be served by publicly virtuous administrators capable of being effectively superintended by public opinion. It is to the possible remedies of this condition that we now turn.

5

Educating the Governors

Historically, one usually finds considerable disagreement as to what a proper education should be for the people who would govern in any given regime. Such educations are, by definition, "political" in that, at a minimum, they seek to hone rationality at the same time that they channel the passions and interests of the individual toward higher ends. The elevated goal may be simply the creation of an ideal citizen dedicated to advancing the common interests of the regime. Achieving this state, however, traditionally required repression, for the regimes—at least those that preceded America—were not interested in liberating the individual. Thus, one of the more extreme examples of political education is provided by Lycurgus, who set out to produce the finest warriors the world had ever seen. The Spartan education revered maleness, denigrated almost everything that was female, suppressed money and commerce, made education a thoroughly public matter (which began at age seven when the boys were removed from female influence and sent to camps), and in general praised all efforts that contributed to military prowess.[1]

Yet not all (or even many) regimes were willing or able to go quite so far to produce exemplary citizens devoted to one goal: action. Undoubtedly one of the most famous and extensive alternatives to the Spartan regime is provided by Plato's *Republic,* which sought ("in speech") to design an ideal education for both governors and governed. The philosophers ultimately would rule, for both the regime and those citizens who were capable were dedicated to the pursuit of wisdom and truth. Preparation for ruling required having one's natural suitability detected early and then nurtured by an appropriately rigorous physical, poetic, and philosophic education. Sexual inequalities were minimized. But this was, after all, only a regime "in speech"; the likelihood that it would become a reality was in the decidedly fickle hands of Chance.

These two modes of preparation for citizenship and governance may exemplify the two poles of political education, one dedicated to a life of action and the other to a life of the mind. Since few rational human beings would voluntarily choose to live in either one of these two regimes, it is probably fortunate that they are either extraordinarily rare (Sparta) or nonexistent (Plato). In a large commercial republic such as our own, we have taken the prudent, logical course: we have compromised (but in some interesting and somewhat unique ways). To have a standard against which to measure our contemporary approach to education for both governors and governed, it is necessary to have a basic understanding of several factors, including the emphasis of our current approach, the two principal educational influences—classical republicanism and the ideas of Locke—that were most enticing to our own Founders, and the proposals for the preparation of future governors that were championed by such thoughtful Founders as Jefferson and Franklin.

CONTEMPORARY PREPARATION

For some time now America has been engaged in a major political debate about the kind and quality of education received by the vast majority of its citizens. Distressed by the extensive failures of a universal system of public education that once was the regime's great pride (for it took immense numbers of diverse individuals and gave them literacy along with a common appreciation of the ideals and history of the nation), citizens are now calling for major reforms. Should the schools be privatized? Should home schooling be protected and encouraged? Should vouchers be given to public schoolchildren and their parents permitted to choose whatever schools best suit their needs?

The urge for reform extends beyond citizen education to the education of our governors. Savvy parents, for example, have always understood that there were some well-traveled educational routes to governance in America. Graduation from one of the nation's elite Ivy League colleges—especially if coupled with shrewd employment and public service choices thereafter—was commonly seen as one such avenue to high elective or appointive office. Yet it is precisely the undemocratic features of this route (and the obvious corollary that it produces governors quite unlike the electorate at large) that have given rise to growing protests about the suitability of such individuals to govern.[2]

Although the debate is likely to continue for some time about who should govern at the highest levels of our regime (along with the closely related question about what is to be considered the proper preparation for such governance), we are in a rather unique position when it comes to discussion of the desired qualifications for those 16 million citizens who, as public employees, collectively wield that critical political power of "administrative discretion."

In America we seem to have reached a rather firm consensus that, in order to serve the citizenry well, the people who will administer our laws and regulations should have a thorough grounding in certain core subjects. Hence, we offer specialized training in the field of public administration, with a heavy emphasis on postbaccalaureate studies leading to a master's degree in public administration. One could argue that the contemporary education we provide for the students going through these various public administration programs is really quite in keeping with Publius's promise of a new "science of politics."[3] Reflecting the desire within the field that it be a true profession (and, perhaps, still more than a little influenced by the original Wilsonian contention that a politics/administration dichotomy exists), these programs emphasize subjects that not only are as scientific as possible and but that also have clear practical applications. Programs adopting the standards of the field's premier accrediting body, the National Association of Schools of Public Affairs and Administration (NASPAA), offer a set of core courses in three separate areas: Management of Public Service Organizations, Application of Quantitative and Qualitative Techniques of Analysis, and Understanding of the Public Policy and Organizational Environment.[4]

Although sound programs may have as one of their missions the laudable goal of familiarizing their students with the full range of the "social, economic, political, and legal contexts of public . . . agency administration,"[5] these contexts are too often seen as being outside the core concerns of the field. Hence, it is not uncommon for fundamental courses on public law, administrative theory, and ethics to be relegated to the status of electives, particularly in programs with a strong public management orientation.

Unlike the model once firmly entrenched in Great Britain (where prospective administrators, having received a strong liberal arts education, essentially acquired experiential knowledge about public administration through carefully structured exposure on the job), the American view has been that there is a special body of knowledge that needs to be acquired formally. The British model presumed that the appropriate regime values were acquired before one ever entered the public service; the American model can only hope that this is the case. If (as has now occurred) this hope comes to be seen as having been too optimistic, the contemporary response generally has been to emphasize ethical codes of conduct. (One of the more extreme examples of this response is the Federal Office of Governmental Ethics, which is charged with supervising the regular teaching of ethics to public servants in the executive branch.)

Is this contemporary focus on a practical education based in "useful" kinds of knowledge a logical derivative of Publius's "new science of politics?" Is teaching *about* ethics an inevitable consequence of the Founders' deliberate decision to foster lifestyles rather than a way of life? If one considers the kinds of education some of the Founders thought would be most appropriate for the citizenry of the new regime—and most especially for those citizens who would be charged with its governance—the answer to these questions is a muted "not necessarily." While agreeing on the need to teach practical kinds of knowledge, these Founders were surprisingly unanimous on the end of education: to produce virtuous citizens who would serve the public.

THE INFLUENCE OF CLASSICAL REPUBLICANISM

The importance of a proper education for the individuals who would govern in the American regime was attractive to many of the Founders but especially to the Anti-Federalists. For them the ideal model was the small republic, which was seen as a school of citizenship that nurtured desirable traits such as responsibility, patriotism, and military prowess. (This latter trait historically was considered to be of great importance in the ancient world. Not only was "political courage"—standing firm in the face of mortal danger, if only out of the fear of being considered inadequate in the eyes of one's fellow citizen-soldiers—achievable by the average citizen, but indeed most small democracies found themselves frequently either at war or, at least, preparing for war.[6]) Of course, the nurturing of these desirable traits generally required some conditions that were going to be difficult to accommodate in the new regime.

For instance, classical democratic thought emphasized that both the extent of territory and the number of inhabitants should be limited. Territorial size was important because the citizens were expected to come together and literally be "self-ruling." As a form of "direct democracy," the citizens had to be able to meet in ways and places that were convenient; hence, small geographic size was considered to be a prerequisite. Similarly, since the relatively small number of inhabitants facilitated their ability to know each other (at least by sight), shame served as a restraint on the actions of those people who, though insufficiently self-governed themselves, still cared about what others thought of them. Such a negative restraint may not have made individuals care for a particularly desirable virtue itself, but it at least made them act as if they did.[7] In addition to the physical difficulties imposed by limiting the territory and population of a classical republic, there was the inescapable issue that the inculcation of its civic virtues historically had required coercive measures, that is, the virtues had to be linked with the power of law. In a regime that was already heavily influenced by the Lockean theory of individual rights and acquisitiveness, it was not hard to see the incompatibilities.

Still, a number of the Anti-Federalists proposed the establishment of such institutions as schools or seminaries where youth could be educated in the habits of public virtue. Citizens, they argued, should be broadly educated in morality and the useful arts and sciences. Properly applied (a matter about which there was ample reason to be skeptical in the new regime), such education could form virtuous citizens who, "instead of abusing, would wade up to their knees in blood, to defend their governments."[8]

THE INFLUENCE OF JOHN LOCKE

The Federalists, of course, were similarly interested in the education of the regime's future leaders. They hoped to foster the habits of public virtue through a combination of public and private sources of education. At least indirectly, certain aspects of John Locke's commentaries on education are clearly reflected in some of their thinking. Understanding some of the key elements of Locke's educational thought may help in tracing their later manifestations in the proposals of the Founders and, equally important, in realizing why some interesting ideas were not implemented.

In a way that is quite consistent with the political principles advanced in the second of *The Two Treatises of Government*, Locke stressed the character-forming functions of the family. Far from embracing the coercive power of either the government or the law to form the public virtues of the citizenry, Locke relied exclusively on the private realm. In an approach diametrically opposed to that of the Spartans, Locke's proposal required that boys be kept in the home and, for all practical purposes, educated with the girls. Besides being congruent with his political principle that, at least in the beginning, all human beings were equal, home schooling would seem to promote similar educations for both boys and girls. (The traditional emphasis on a feminine education in home economics and a masculine education in public matters—history, commerce, mathematics—would seem difficult to sustain under these conditions.)

Moreover, on the assumption that only the wealthy upper class could employ the expensive tutors recommended by Locke, much of the responsibility for this type of education ultimately would fall on the mother in middle-class families. As one of only two people (the parents) who reliably could be expected to have the best interests of the young children in the forefronts of their minds, the mother would have to be sufficiently well educated to supervise her son's (and daughter's) education. In other words, she herself would have to have an education nearly the equal of her husband's.[9]

Though having clear practical implications for improving the education of all one's children, in reality this proposal was especially directed at the kind of education potential governors would receive. Female children might enjoy a more equal education under their parents' benign tutelage, but the male was still more likely to end up pursuing positions of power and influence. As a consequence, Locke urged the class of gentlemen to use certain methods to instill appropriate public virtues in their offspring during the childhood years.

Even though civil law and religion have roles to play in morality, Locke thought that the socially derived standards of public opinion more powerfully affected individual conduct, including one's choice of occupations. Therefore, he stressed the need to educate children in the standards or opinions of the community. This early socialization would teach not only the standards but also the idea of rewards or penalties associated with actions that uphold or violate them. In Locke's scheme, a successful education of this sort would control even those individuals who might otherwise casually break religious and civil law in the pursuit of self-interest.[10]

It follows that governments, even though they are legitimately constituted by Lockean standards, will be ineffective unless they rest on a foundation of sound opinion. That in turn can be accomplished only if the content of public opinion is established through the proper education of those citizens on whom the proper functioning of the commonwealth depends.[11]

Locke's argument relies on the assumption that people are by nature acquisitive, ambitious, and self-interested. The task of a proper education, therefore, is not to change human nature but to help channel it in socially beneficial directions.[12] This means, above all, an emphatically practical education—one in which reason is indeed honed but is decidedly in the service of the body. For Locke, there was no emphasis on Platonic wisdom and truth; this was to be an education oriented toward the production of wealth (comfortable self-preservation) and its attendant occupations. Accordingly, education properly conceived should be a process devoted to demonstrating the connections between public virtues and personal rewards. The pursuit of self-interest properly understood is a hallmark of Locke's well-educated gentleman.[13]

Not surprisingly, the Federalists shared Locke's goals (but not all his methods) for the education of the citizenry.

> The major thrust of their activities would be toward the acquisition of property, whether through the careful management of land or through trade, commerce, or such professions as law, medicine, or the like. Their Lockean education would have afforded them considerable scope for the application of their carefully nurtured native intelligence to the broadest possible variety of practical affairs. They would be "men of business," in the broad seventeenth-century meaning of that term.[14]

A PUBLIC LOCKEAN EDUCATION

However attractive some of Locke's educational proposals may have seemed to the Founders, there was one inescapable source of general tension: Locke was clearly directing his thoughts to the British monarchical system. At least for the initial periods, his emphasis on a private education for the children of the wealthy would primarily affect the elites, that is, the Whigs who would govern. Although it was expected that their influence would trickle down over time, it was not really a proposal for mass education. The lower middle class and the poor could only hope to adopt a mere shadow of the education provided by the expensive tutors.[15]

The American regime was unquestionably a republic, and even though some of the Founders from the aristocratic South may have personally benefited from a private Lockean education on the plantations, the new nation could not rely on such methods to produce future governors. Indeed, this monarchical form of education was not well suited for a large commercial republic.

As Locke realized, a privatization of education certainly kept the children from the clutches of the two ancient competitors for the young: the City and the Philosopher. Yet cloistering the young at home also drastically reduced their exposure to models of probity and virtue who might be worthy of emulation. The homogenizing effects of properly established public schools, however, could be of considerable value to a commercial republic, especially in providing "valuable incentives to study and excellent exercises for learning how to compete in a humane and fair spirit."[16] Of equal value to such a republic would be the reinforcement the law receives from a properly constituted public education.

> Lawfully established educational institutions lend to education the majesty of the law and the moral authority of governmental suasion; the whole moral weight of the community is thrown behind education, with profoundly encouraging effects on the outlook of both children and parents.[17]

Furthermore, a private education of the kind Locke advocated provides neither similar educational experiences nor the opportunity to forge mutually reinforcing youthful friendships—the kind in which like souls are attracted to each other because they share similar traits—that can thrive throughout a lifetime. Even in the mid-eighteenth century, it was abundantly evident that the Lockean proposal would need modifications if its particular advantages were going to be adapted to the requirements of the American regime.

The slaveholding culture of the South certainly produced a civil society that was as rigidly stratified as any found in many a traditional monarchy or aristocracy, but Locke's class-based model was nonetheless inadequate for the expected fluidity of America as a whole. The numerous and vibrant social, economic, and political interchanges required of this emphatically commercial republic were going to need a unifying civic glue. Since the classical republican solution of universal military service was impractical (it was not only coercive but also ill-suited to a nation that laid its foundation in the principles of individual freedoms and rights), the advantages to be derived from the alternative of a public system of education were understandably attractive.[18]

THOMAS JEFFERSON AND EDUCATION

Thomas Jefferson's ideas regarding education are significant in part because they are based on a treatment of self-interest that is somewhat at odds with that of Locke. In his *Notes on the State of Virginia,* Jefferson considered his law establishing an educational system in the state to be one of his most important contributions. It fulfilled the need for a public education that would prepare the people to defend their liberty against those individuals who would seek to establish a new form of monarchy.[19] To ensure a sound defense against ambitious despots, he thought the government should provide for the basic education of the people.[20]

> I think our governments will remain virtuous for many centuries; *as long as they are chiefly agricultural.* . . . Above all things I hope the education of the common people will be attended to; convinced that on their good sense we may rely with the most security for the preservation of a due degree of liberty.[21]

It was from among these educated citizens that Jefferson hoped to find the best qualified governors to serve each successive generation. Contending that "people will be happiest whose laws are best, and are best administered, and that laws will be wisely formed, and honestly administered, in proportion as those who form and administer them are wise and honest," Jefferson set forth a plan to discover those "fitly formed" children "whom nature had endowed with genius and virtue."[22] After a selection process that grew progressively more rigorous as the students advanced in their studies, those few students possessing the most superior "parts and disposition" were to be sent on for three years of studying science at William and Mary College. Upon graduation, these college students were to serve the state.[23]

This plan contained two features that were to be relatively common elements of public education until fairly recent times. The first was the insistence that the purpose of public education was to produce fitly formed democratic citizens who would serve the regime. This purpose recognized that the children being publicly educated today were going to become the voting citizens of tomorrow. They would elect the governors and influence the policies of the nation. This was no small responsibility, but the purpose of public education was actually aiming beyond fostering such good citizenship. As Jefferson so clearly stated, it sought to identify and nurture individuals who by nature were suited to govern. Although the education of the citizens as citizens was wholly compatible with the powerful principles of equality that undergirded the regime, the selection of naturally superior future governors introduced an element of tension. Indeed, such a publicly educated natural aristocracy had clear antecedents in the classical republican models. (It even had striking similarities to the Spartan program advocated by Lycurgus.) Jefferson nevertheless fully appreciated the potential advantages to be derived from properly drawing upon the naturally gifted:

> The natural aristocracy I consider as the most precious gift of nature, for the instruction, the trusts, and government of society. And indeed it would have been inconsistent in creation to

have formed man for the social state, and not to have provided virtue and wisdom enough to manage the concerns of the society. May we not even say that that form of government is the best which provides the most effectually for a pure selection of these natural aristoi into the offices of government?[24]

From Jefferson's perspective, however, this reliance on a carefully cultivated meritocracy had a limit, and it blended nicely with the regime's principles of equality.

The principal author of the Declaration of Independence had a lifelong distrust of people in power. Furthermore, he was quite wary of the belief that structural impediments could long substitute for the citizenry's possession of a solid republican character. His advocacy of both a natural aristocracy of governors and a broad education of the citizenry came together in a typically Lockean remedy. Jefferson made a crucial distinction between urging that the virtuous and naturally qualified be channeled into public service and the quite different contention that these individuals were somehow intended by nature to rule. (After all, it was Jefferson who emphatically stated that "the mass of mankind has not been born with saddles on their backs, nor a favored few booted and spurred, ready to ride them legitimately, by the grace of God."[25]) Rather, the educated citizenry was expected to watch the governors as a firm bulwark against the latter's corruption. Indeed, by being both aware of and attuned to the citizenry's watchfulness, such governors are virtually restrained by a Lockean concern for public opinion. In return, they would serve the citizens in the way Jefferson thought most appropriate: as diligent guardians who would see to it that the citizenry's Lockean natural rights are as well secured as possible.

A few years before his death Jefferson had a final occasion to further the cause of citizen education in his "Report of the Commissioners to Fix the Site of the University of Virginia, August 1, 1818," an extensive plan for establishing a public institution of higher learning. In it he makes a distinction between the objectives of primary and higher education. The former seeks to provide every citizen with the basic information needed to transact business, the ability to calculate, an improvement of "morals and faculties," an understanding of duties and rights, and the ability intelligently and faithfully to observe "all the social relations under which he shall be placed." The latter seeks, first and foremost, to form "the statesmen, legislators and judges"; to teach the "principles and structure of government"; to "harmonize and promote the interests of agriculture, manufactures and commerce"; to develop "the reasoning faculties of our youth, enlarge their minds, cultivate their morals, and instill into them the precepts of virtue and order"; to "enlighten them with mathematical and physical sciences"; and to "form them to habits of reflection and correct action." The purpose, though, was manifest: the "incalculable advantage of training up able counsellors to administer the affairs of our country in all its departments . . . and to bear their proper share in the councils of our national government."[26]

BENJAMIN FRANKLIN AND EDUCATION

Thomas Jefferson and Benjamin Franklin shared mutual interests, a deep and abiding dedication to the principles of republican rule, and minds that were especially receptive to scientific inquiry. It is not surprising, therefore, to find that Franklin also gave considerable thought to the subject of an appropriate education for the citizens of America. Indeed, although his writings on education are not quite as extensive as Jefferson's, they predated them and are even more obviously Lockean in their origins.

Franklin thought that there was only one "end of education, virtue, which he defines as service to one's fellowman."[27] The history of the northeastern United States (especially New England, New York, and Pennsylvania) had long showed a deep appreciation for classically inspired educations that also had solid religious elements.[28] Franklin's approach deemphasized immersion in religion in favor of a "civic religion" taught in conjunction with history. In essence, this approach was to be "the minimal popular creed which history showed to be essential for social health."[29]

Allowing exceptions for those relatively few individuals seeking the traditional callings (divinity, law, medicine), Franklin's formula also emphasized the mastery of one's own language, English, over classical Greek and Latin. As Franklin understood:

> The study of dead or even foreign languages played no role whatsoever in Greek civic education. . . . What was important for the classical citizen, in contrast to the later classical grammarians and scholars, was less belles lettres than the development of the capacities appropriate to an economically independent and public-spirited member of society.[30]

The development of graceful prose and oral skills in English were clearly essential to citizens in a self-governing regime. So too were the kinds of practical knowledge (natural history or science, commerce, "mechanical philosophy") that would prepare these young men for life in their commercial republic.

The content of the proposed education may have owed much to Locke, but the manner in which it would be conducted did not. Franklin advocated the establishment of boarding "academies" where the young boys could be separated from the influences of their families and receive the benefit of a common educational experience. The academies could be funded by wealthy, civic-minded patrons and scholarships provided for the well-qualified children of parents who were otherwise too poor to bear the costs. In this environment virtue could be fostered (through emulation especially) and the principal end of education best achieved: the preparation of virtuous young men who would go forth and serve their regime.

EDUCATION AND PUBLIC VIRTUE

Thus, in tandem with the establishment of such principles as constitutional correctives and the encouragement of honor, education was an integral part of the Founders' attempts to better ensure that the American regime would be served by publicly virtuous governors. One hundred years later, Woodrow Wilson was to make this connection between education and virtue a key element of his famous essay on public administration. Of course, he did not believe that "universal political education" would in itself create the kind of public administrators that were needed. In 1887, governance required the sort of technical training that probably would have met with some measure of approval from Franklin and Jefferson: "It will be necessary to organize democracy by sending up to the competitive examinations for the civil service men definitely prepared for standing liberal tests as to technical knowledge. A technically schooled civil service will presently become indispensable."[31] Dwight Waldo later observed that Wilson "saw everything through a political lens . . . and was highly motivated to make the republican-democratic [experiment] succeed."[32] However, Wilson's lecture notes reveal that he had no intention of restricting public administration education to purely instrumental or technical matters. Constitutional principles, history, comparative government, practical politics, public law, and management were essential to a proper curriculum.[33] And it is within this context that Wilson described his goal: "The ideal for us is a civil service cultured and self-sufficient enough to act with sense and vigor, and yet so intimately connected with the popular thought, by means of elections and constant public counsel, as to find arbitrariness or class spirit quite out of the question."[34]

6

The American Character and Public Policy

The issue of the proper place and function of American public administration must now be examined from a slightly different perspective; namely, what kinds of public policies are most compatible with the character of the citizenry? Using both political and economic arguments, critics of the modern administrative state see it as undermining those character traits upon which the Founders relied.[1] Big government and its bureaucratic apparatus are accused of being particularly prone to self-serving practices that undermine liberty. Government insurance, welfare, and regulatory programs are portrayed as eroding self-reliance and individual initiative.[2] Liberal thought, however (especially that of Madison and Hamilton), is in several key ways quite supportive of positive government and of its associated administrative activities.[3] Moreover, liberal concepts and Founding principles may be used both to support or to defend American public administration as well as to suggest its proper limits. In order to illustrate these points, I have selected several major New Deal programs that are usually considered to be departures from Founding intentions.

* * *

FOUNDING THOUGHT AND
THE AMERICAN CHARACTER

The Founders (either implicitly or explicitly) considered several character traits to be integral to the American regime.[4] Among the more important were individualism, acquisitiveness, and reputation.

Individualism—The democratic character is self-centered to the point that the "private world" is considered to be more important than the general welfare as a guide to behavior. The individual is expected to assess various political and economic choices according to how well they might contribute to the improvement of his own conditions. The Founders successfully argued for a republic on the grounds that individualism was a predictable, if not uplifting, trait whose negative features might better be controlled through a managed clash of interests than by a reliance on the regime's capacity to reform the individual.[5]

Acquisitiveness—Although low or base in comparison to such Aristotelian virtues as magnanimity or liberality, this trait is intrinsic to the American character set forth in Founding thought. In the tradition of Locke and Smith, Madison believed that acquisitiveness served as a moral code for the commercial society because to be successful one must take risks, exercise self-discipline, maintain a reputation for honesty, be industrious, and often be willing to delay gratification.[6]

Reputation—The democratic character is quite image-oriented. Appropriate behavior is generally defined externally, that is, by others whose opinions are seen to be important for both self-regarding and instrumental reasons. The opinions of one's peers and neighbors are attended to because they are important to self-image; instrumentally, reputation is valued because it is believed to have economic and political consequences. As citizens and actors in the marketplace, democrats seek to avoid the shame attached to violations of conventional norms. Behavior is self-controlled to the extent that the individual is responsive to public praise and condemnation, but the standards are set externally by "reference groups."[7]

These three character traits, though necessary to sustain a regime that is both democratic and commercial, are, as James Madison recognized, a comparatively low moral foundation upon which to build a republic. This criticism is often made by those people who believe that the regime and its citizens would benefit (in ethical if not material terms) from seeking more noble ends.[8] Yet the Madisonian point of view, which accepts the modern image of human nature as essentially self-interested, continues to be the best-known summary statement on the accommodation of these traits by the political institutions of the American regime. Thus, in the course of discussing ways in which the governors would be impeded from taking advantage of the governed, Madison argues in *Federalist* No. 51 that

the interest of the man must be connected with the constitutional rights of the place. It may be a reflection on human nature, that such devices should be necessary to control the abuses of government. But what is government itself, but the greatest of all reflections on human nature? If men were angels, no government would be necessary. If angels were to govern men, neither external nor internal controls on government would be necessary. . . . A dependence on the people is, no doubt, the primary control on the government; but experience has taught mankind the necessity of auxiliary precautions.[9]

In contrast to the classical concept of the *polis,* which saw the regime as a comprehensive system for the formation of character, the Madisonian argument relies on the tradition of Machiavelli, Hobbes, and Locke.[10] As Martin Diamond commented, these "auxiliary precautions" were to assist in reorienting mankind away from the ancient concentration on character formation. Instead, the "realistic task" was to channel "man's passions and interests toward the achievement of those solid goods this earth has to offer."[11] An important feature of the consequent new (liberal) tradition is the extent to which the state and the society are separated. The classical approach entertained no such arrangement, but liberalism explicitly creates a large realm of "private" character-forming institutions, among the most important of which are certainly family, church, and school. The liberal state or government is assumed to have a secondary (although not insignificant) role in the process of forming the characters of its citizens.[12]

THE ADMINISTRATIVE STATE AND THE AMERICAN CHARACTER

Americans have long considered Alexis de Tocqueville to be one of the earliest and most insightful observers of our regime. When the nation was barely two generations old, Tocqueville came with the ultimate purpose of understanding the intricate workings of the system the Founders had established. Because of the remarkable acuity and endurance of his insights, Tocqueville's works are often cited by those individuals critical of the welfare or regulatory state's impact on the character of the American people.[13] For instance, Tocqueville is well known for his statement that, as a democratic people become more equal, there is a greater need for them to rely on the government and its administrative agencies, with the result that they become less and less free.[14]

> Many of my contemporaries . . . claim that as the citizens become weaker and more helpless, the government must become proportionately more skillful and active, so that society should do what is no longer possible for individuals . . . but I think they are mistaken.
>
> A government could take the place of some of the largest associations in America. . . . But what political power could ever carry on the vast multitude of lesser undertakings which associations daily enable American citizens to control?

It is easy to see the time coming in which men will be less and less able to produce, by each alone, the commonest bare necessities of life. The tasks of government must therefore perpetually increase, and its efforts to cope with them must spread its net ever wider. The more government takes the place of associations, the more will individuals lose the idea of forming associations and need the government to come to their help. That is a vicious circle of cause and effect. *Must the public administration cope with every industrial undertaking beyond the competence of one individual citizen?* . . . The morals and intelligence of a democratic people would be in as much danger as its commerce and industry if ever a government wholly usurped the place of private associations.[15]

In current terms, Tocqueville alerts us to at least two perils threatening the citizens' virtues and habits necessary to an effective democracy: as government expands, individuals increasingly will become dependent and passive; and greater dependency will encourage the government's assumption of responsibilities that previously were performed by voluntary or private associations.[16] According to Tocqueville, in the absence of government action, individuals must of necessity provide (however inadequately) for their own needs (social, security, spiritual, and material) through either their own efforts or those of voluntary associations they have freely joined. Given the modern administrative state's emphasis on welfare and regulatory functions, Tocqueville's observation is particularly meaningful because he posits a direct relationship between the citizens' capacity for political liberty and the extent to which they depend on government. In his analysis, political and economic liberty is fostered by voluntary associations among citizens acting within a framework of decentralized government. On the other hand, liberty is threatened by democracy's tendency to centralize power (in this case state and federal power). Tocqueville was quite aware that this centralizing process might well threaten democracy itself, clearing the way for despotism.

When conditions are unequal, no inequality, however great, offends the eye. But amid general uniformity, the slightest dissimilarity seems shocking, and the completer the uniformity, the more unbearable it seems. It is therefore natural that love of equality should grow constantly with equality itself; everything done to satisfy it makes it grow. . . . Every central power which follows its natural instincts loves equality and favors it. For equality singularly facilitates, extends, and secures its influence. One can also assert that every central government worships uniformity; uniformity saves it the trouble of inquiring into infinite details, which would be necessary if the rules were made to suit men instead of subjecting all men indiscriminately to the same rule. Hence the government loves what the citizens love, and it naturally hates what they hate.[17]

Tocqueville's analysis is paralleled in the political thought of John Locke and Adam Smith. Both men stressed what they saw to be vital connections between the free market, citizen character, and political liberty.[18] In their analyses, the market is a character-forming institution that produces rugged individualists who understand and pursue their own interests. Yet the market also tames the acquisitive individual and limits his opportunities to do major harm to society. (As Samuel Johnson remarked in a letter to William Strahan: "There are few ways in which a man can be more innocently employed than in getting money."[19]) This social control is achieved without resort to coercive hierarchies and imposed definitions of the public interest because the market

is a social system which does not depend for its functioning on our finding good men for running it, or on all men becoming better than they are now, but which makes use of men in all their given variety and complexity, sometimes good and sometimes bad, sometimes intelligent and more often stupid.[20]

Following this line of reasoning, governmental interference in the normal operations of the market poses at least an indirect threat to liberty and the social order by impeding the development of individualism and by breaking down the market's capacity to discipline behavior.

Accordingly, contemporary critics such as Milton Friedman would restrict government's proper functions to "the maintenance of law and order to prevent coercion of one individual by another, the enforcement of contracts voluntarily entered into, the definition of the meaning of property rights, the interpretation and enforcement of such rights, and the provision of a monetary framework."[21] Additionally, he assigns to the free market a major role in the development and protection of political liberty:

> Viewed as a means to the end of political freedom, economic arrangements are important because of their effect on the concentration or dispersion of power. The kind of economic organization that provides economic freedom directly, namely, competitive capitalism, also promotes political freedom because it separates economic power from political power and in this way enables the one to offset the other. . . .Historical evidence speaks with a single voice on the relation between political freedom and the free market. I know of no example in time or place of a society that has been marked by a large measure of political freedom, and that has not also used something comparable to a free market to organize the bulk of economic activity.[22]

For Friedman, George Gilder, Thomas Sowell, and other widely read commentators who share this perspective, it is the market that requires and reinforces the behaviors and attitudes that are essential to democracy, to liberty, and ultimately, to the regime envisioned by the Founders.[23] Madison, for example, argued that diversity in the "kinds and degrees" of property found in a commercial regime causes the self-interested majority to fragment into various contending factions, thereby decreasing the likelihood that it would be able to oppress minorities.[24]

George Gilder, whose efforts to blend some of the tenets of Christianity with those of market economics apparently influenced some members of the former Reagan administration, asserts that welfare is morally debilitating and incapable of supporting the energy and imagination needed to sustain capitalism and democracy.[25] Insofar as the American character is concerned, Gilder sees great moral hazards associated with government's acting to shield the citizenry against risk. He concludes that "much evidence . . . indicates . . . that the [welfare] programs have surprisingly little beneficial effect, but they do have a dramatic negative impact on motivation and self-reliance."[26] In the final analysis, the security offered by the administrative state's welfare activities comes at a high price: the destruction of liberty and the crippling of the society's capacity to produce wealth.

THE CORRECTIVE FUNCTIONS OF THE REGIME

There are also individuals who see the regime as the primary influence on the life of the citizen, however. In its extreme form, this tradition, with intellectual roots in the works of Plato and Aristotle, stresses a need to establish hierarchical relationships between the rulers and the ruled.[27] In effect, enlightened governors assume responsibility for and power over major aspects of the citizens' economic, political, social, and spiritual lives. Considerable faith is placed in the wisdom of political leaders and in the capacities of administrative officials as well as of technical experts to achieve the public interest.[28] This view explicitly joins "truth" and power and, in so doing, makes hierarchy an organizing principle.[29] Since the attainment of collective or public goods is emphasized, individualism and self-interested acquisitiveness are treated as character flaws that are serious threats to any properly constituted regime.[30] Whereas the liberal regime operates on the assumption that generally character will be formed and virtues acquired in the private realm, regimes based on hierarchical precepts make character formation a public matter and, in practice, devote considerable resources to this process.[31]

In the United States, the hierarchical perspective has had a considerable (but greatly democratized) influence. Most notably, it has found expression in the ideas of those individuals who, while generally supportive of democracy and capitalism, urge a heavier reliance on state planning and regulation as socially and politically necessary correctives to the excesses of majoritarian politics and unrestrained free markets and who maintain that government is the only modern institution capable of ensuring that all citizens will enjoy a certain minimum level of security and will have the opportunity to better themselves. Implied in both of these positions is the need for a relatively large public sector made up of administrative agencies staffed by experts who have a major role in determining how these functions will be carried out.

There is little question that the Founders relied heavily on individualism and acquisitiveness as the primary bases for a commercial democratic republic. But they also thought that these traits had to be supplemented by certain hierarchical arrangements because, by itself, acquisitive individualism was an insufficient foundation for the proposed regime. They saw the unrestrained pursuit of self-interest that is intrinsic to simple majoritarian politics and free markets as a threat to liberty and to republican government. Consequently, they sought reliable mechanisms by which public and private interests might be successfully joined.[32] As they anticipated, the search for these devices has proven to be one of the most difficult and enduring problems faced by American leaders.

Thus, such a strong exponent of American democracy and individualism as Tocqueville was well aware of their problematic features: "Individualism is a calm and considered feeling which disposes each citizen to isolate himself from the mass of his fellows and withdraw into the circle of family and friends; with this little society formed to his taste, he gladly leaves the greater society to look after itself."[33] Though considering individualism to be a key component in a properly constituted democratic regime and a necessary element of a free market, Tocqueville also recognized that it must be controlled or channeled because it may otherwise threaten the common interest. However, he did not believe that American individualism was a fundamental character flaw that required coercive state remedies but that "it is due more to inadequate understanding than to perversity of heart."[34] In his opinion, the American citizen could learn to understand the connections between self-interest and the general interest through day-to-day participation in the management of public affairs.[35]

Nevertheless, the Founders did not rely completely on the capacity of a democratic republic to educate and moderate the individual. They established a constitutional basis for administrative controls of those relatively few individuals who refuse to restrain their pursuit of self-interest even when the general welfare is threatened or who cannot, for whatever reason, comprehend the public interest.[36]

Managing or channeling the clashes between public and private interests is certainly not a problem unique to democratic regimes. All regimes have had to deal with human nature, either by attempting to change it or by accommodating it. Nevertheless, the American solution is unusual in that it was premised upon the assumption that acquisitive individualism could be a solid foundation for the regime—*if* certain institutional and political conditions existed. The Founders were well aware that simply "emancipating acquisitiveness" could have potentially fatal consequences, and they sought to minimize the risks by devising a large, commercial republic that insulated the governors from the direct influence of factions.[37] The Constitution of this republic diffuses power between levels and branches of government, but it also carefully specifies that federal law shall be supreme. Hamilton, who wanted even stronger controls on popular impulses, saw to it that the federal government would have the constitutional authority to be an active participant in and, when required, a regulator of such matters as interstate commerce.[38] In short, it was intended that American government have the capacity to correct the undesirable consequences of individualism and acquisitiveness. Moreover, to be effective, this corrective function does not require rule by an enlightened political aristocracy or an administrative elite.

> Not many of the Framers were quite as confident as [James] Wilson of the reasonableness of the people, but the government they constructed was nevertheless understood by them all to be unusual in the relatively small demands it placed on

a political aristocracy and in the relatively great demands it placed on the people.[39]

In addition to incorporating the institutional correctives of individualism and acquisitiveness, the Founders also understood how important it was to have a population that learned the "civic virtues" required to sustain the Republic. Martin Diamond observes that the Founding is "itself an ethical admonition," an exercise in "declaratory tutelage," and "a gentle instruction in civic values."[40] Yet the Founders were cautious men; to these indirect methods they added a capacity for direct and not always gentle discipline. Those public administrators who apply some of this discipline often must combine the powers and responsibilities of the three constitutional branches.[41] And major arguments over the legitimacy of the power wielded by public administrators have periodically arisen. Despite these concerns about the emergence of a large bureaucratic establishment, it is still a logical (albeit controversial) product of the constitutional framework.[42]

PUBLIC POLICY AND THE AMERICAN REGIME

In their efforts to bridge public and private interests within the framework of the regime, American public administrators cannot proceed on the assumption that individualism and acquisitiveness are vices that should not be tolerated, much less accommodated. Nor can they legitimately retreat from a responsibility to promote the general welfare and to protect the regime. The Founders intended that certain correctives serve to link public and private interests, not substitute one for the other. This admittedly difficult function requires public administrators to work actively to uphold the character traits that are central to the regime and to be alert to the ways in which administrative programs may be used to encourage citizens to see how their self-interest may be related to broader public interests.[43] The Great Depression and the Roosevelt administration's policy responses to it provide dramatic examples of efforts to expand the scope of American public administration greatly while still remaining supportive of those character traits that underpin Founding principles. FDR's approach continues to embody a number of useful guidelines that are applicable to the practice of American public administration today. In 1931, Roosevelt discussed the state and its duties:

> What is the State? It is the duly constituted representative of an organized society of human beings, created by them for their mutual protection and well-being. "The State" or "The Government" is but the machinery through which such mutual aid and protection are achieved. . . .
>
> One of the duties of the State is that of caring for those of its citizens who find themselves the victims of such adverse circumstances as make them unable to obtain even the necessity for mere existence without the aid of others. That responsibility is recognized by every civilized nation. . . .
>
> In broad terms, I assert that modern society, acting through its Government, owes the definite obligation to prevent the starvation or the dire want of any of its fellow men and women who try to maintain themselves but cannot. . . . To these unfortunate citizens aid must be extended by Government, not as a matter of charity, but as a matter of social duty.[44]

From this relatively modest beginning, over the next twelve years Roosevelt greatly expanded his concept of the role government should play in ensuring the security of the American citizen. By 1944 he had set forth a legislative agenda, a new "bill of rights," containing the following goals: (1) jobs for all who wanted them; (2) adequate incomes; (3) free and fair trade; (4) decent housing; (5) universal access to medical care and to good health; (6) security from fears of old age, illness, and unemployment; and (7) a good education available to all.[45] FDR informed the Congress:

> We have come to a clear realization of the fact that true individual freedom cannot exist without economic security and

independence. "Necessitous men are not free men." People who are hungry and out of a job are the stuff of which dictatorships are made.[46]

The emphasis on government-provided security, of course, runs counter to the usual interpretation of Tocqueville's thesis, namely, that a welfare state, because of the dependency and passivity it fosters, can only undermine the American regime. Critics of the New Deal's relief programs and of broadly gauged insurance programs such as Social Security have followed this line of reasoning, using it as a mainstay in contemporary attacks on big government and bureaucracy. But a close reading of Tocqueville reveals that there is much to support Roosevelt's position. In this context, the justification for extensive public welfare programs is to be found in Tocqueville's assertion that democracy is threatened by a government that assumes those "lesser" responsibilities that an individual, either singly or through voluntary associations, could be capable of providing for himself. In fact, Tocqueville advises a careful differentiation between what can be done by the individual and what has to be done by government because it is realistically beyond the individual's capabilities.[47] In other words, questions about the proper domain, size, and power of government must be contextually framed and answered.

The United States of 1933 differed greatly from the nation Tocqueville wrote about. The Great Depression exposed the interdependencies of an industrialized and increasingly urban society. The New Dealers recognized that huge numbers of Americans were, in the most fundamental sense of the word, dependent on economic forces and processes that were simply beyond their control. After four years of depression, the national income had dropped over 50 percent, unemployment had reached 25 percent of the labor force, public and private welfare facilities were breaking down, and the banking system was on the verge of collapse. Public confidence in the free enterprise system was badly shaken, and many people, including Roosevelt, believed that democracy itself was threatened.[48] Others, including Herbert Hoover, argued that the economy would "self-correct" and that "rugged individualism" would be destroyed and liberty consequently reduced if the national government implemented extensive relief and welfare programs.[49] Roosevelt's election, though not a mandate for radical change, did signal the electorate's support for a more active federal government. This support did not significantly decline until the mid-1960s.[50] The social welfare programs (and accompanying administrative agencies) of the New Deal stand today as monuments to FDR's vision of a positive liberalism fitted to the social, economic, and political realities confronting the United States during the 1930s.[51] Hubert Humphrey, in a typically enthusiastic manner, described the thrust of New Deal liberalism:

> The New Deal made liberalism a positive force for the betterment of the human condition; it saw freedom as more than the absence of restraint. Freedom was characterized by a better life, better homes, better education. Government was to be more than the protector and the regulator, it was to be a partner, a constructive force, in improving the nation and helping the individual.[52]

Humphrey's New Deal liberalism is now being severely criticized by opponents, who argue that the welfare state's role as the administrator of a comprehensive Social Security system must be severely scaled down in order to restore American individualism and self-sufficiency. If Tocqueville's prescription that government should take on responsibilities only when individuals and voluntary associations are not able to handle them is to be followed, legislators and administrators should be prepared to evaluate existing programs accordingly. Roosevelt, for example, argued convincingly that redefinitions of individual self-sufficiency and responsibility were needed because the national government faced an economic crisis with which millions of Americans were effectively unable to cope. The New Deal response therefore did not appear to violate Tocqueville's precepts. From this perspective, these precepts are still as useful as they were in Tocqueville's day. At a minimum, they require that critical evaluations of government's role in the political, social, and economic affairs of the regime be carefully performed. Although much of the responsibility for this kind of evaluation must fall to elected officials, it also requires the kind of nondoctrinaire analysis and technical expertise that public administrators should be able to provide.

SOME DERIVED POLICY GUIDELINES

The American regime was intended by the Founders to have an extensive system of political and economic (or market) controls that would constrain the actions of both governed and governors. Because these arrangements are, to a considerable extent, self-regulating and well fitted to the American character, they escape the tensions normally associated with their administratively imposed alternatives. However, since they are demonstrably imperfect as ways of governing a regime as diverse and complex as ours, certain hierarchical correctives (such as federalism, the judiciary, the regulation of commerce) are essential. Other supplementary correctives, including insurance and subsidy programs, emergency relief, and public enterprise, also may be necessary. An important problem confronting today's public administrators, therefore, is to devise guidelines for making decisions about whether or not specific hierarchical correctives are needed and then to determine if they are compatible with the long-range interests of the regime. Included among these critical interests must be the effects such correctives would have on American character traits.

It should also be emphasized that policy choices of this sort are not usually between clearly defined and sharply different alternatives. More likely are situations in which legislators, judges, and administrators must select from a range of mixed options. Accordingly, the guidelines I present overlap, and their relative weights and relevance will vary from case to case. The examples are drawn from the New Deal primarily because the Roosevelt administration seemed rather consistently to have followed these guidelines.

Guideline 1: Promote voluntary, self-interested citizen participation in policymaking processes and administrative arrangements that have the capacity to accomplish necessary correctives while encouraging the people involved to see the public interest. As many observers have pointed out, the American public administrator must understand and work within the limitations imposed by the interdependencies and conflicts between bureaucracy and democracy.[53] Although the resulting tensions are probably inevitable, there is no reason to expand the already vast array of opportunities for clashes. At times, forsaking bureaucratic means will entail using forms of organization that have neither the control nor the technical (efficiency) capabilities of a bureaucracy. These kinds of costs must be balanced against possible benefits in at least two areas: the cultivation of individual attitudes, habits, behaviors, and skills that enhance the quality and capacity of American democracy and public support for government in general. Tocqueville, while admitting that individual efforts are "often less successful than authorities," observed that the overall result of "individual strivings amounts to much more than any administration could undertake" and that the beneficial effects on character are very important.[54]

A useful illustration of this guideline is the strategy employed by the Roosevelt administration to begin the process of eliminating a key contributor to the Depression: the economic collapse of American agriculture. The Agricultural Adjustment Act represented an attempt to steer a course between the extremes of an unregulated free market and direct planning and control by the Department of Agriculture. In effect, the act sought to implement a planning process based on a powerful alliance of the Extension Service, the Farm Bureau, and the land grant colleges. Important decisions were made by the farmers through county production-control committees. Especially relevant here is the act's reported impact on the behaviors of the people involved. The act paid farmers to be concerned with the interests of the farming community and, ultimately, with the entire society; they were materially rewarded for voluntarily participating in the planning process. Thus, Arthur Schlesinger describes the act as a device for connecting self-interest with the social good or welfare and as a means of encouraging farmers to see how their individual interests were tied to the needs of the agricultural community at large: "Running their own show within a framework of national policy, they educated themselves in social discipline."[55]

Guideline 2: Seek correctives that tap or exploit key aspects of the American character, particularly acquisitiveness, individualism, and concern for reputation. Perhaps the most ambitious of the New Deal programs was the short-lived National Recovery Administration (NRA). Although it failed to accomplish its purposes and, like the Agricultural Adjustment Act, was eventually ruled unconstitutional by the Supreme Court, it is a fascinating example of Roosevelt's willingness to use public administration as a framework for voluntary, cooperative planning and resource allocation within industries. Central to the depression was a cycle of cutthroat competition that depressed prices, wages, working conditions, and purchasing power. Roosevelt, as he had done in the case of agriculture, accepted the point of view that competition could not be relied upon to protect the public interest. He seized on the NRA as a way of obtaining cooperation, coordination, and responsiveness to the public welfare without resorting to drastic changes in the ownership and management of the nation's industrial base.

Briefly, the NRA operated through codes negotiated within industries that set standards for wages, hours, and working conditions. It supervised code development and approved agreements and was supposed to help enforce them. From a national policy perspective, the codes were intended to stabilize wages and to build purchasing power. Corporate self-interest was to be served by the reversal of the downward spiral of wages, prices, and profits (and the suspension of the Sherman Antitrust Act). Voluntary participation in the code system was expected to be the rule, but the NRA administrators went beyond the inducement of market stability and improved profitability by threatening direct government control if the voluntary approach failed, by publicly honoring industrialists who did join (with the Blue Eagle), and by using public opinion to shame those who did not join.[56] Corporate resistance and evasion were publicly condemned as violations of the basic American virtues of moderation, civility, and courage.

As a comprehensive formula for linking public and private corporate interests within a market economy, the NRA failed; however, it left an impressive legacy of reforms, perhaps most significantly in that "it accustomed the country to the feasibility of government regulation and taught people to think in terms of national policy for business and for labor."[57] More specifically, the NRA process set the stage for subsequent laws controlling working hours and minimum wages, abolishing child labor and the sweatshop system, establishing collective bargaining as a national policy, giving status to consumers, and stamping out a "noxious collection of unfair trade practices."[58]

Guideline 3: Attempt to structure social-economic insurance programs in ways that visibly link the citizens' self-interest to participation and support. Social Security was one of the most controversial of the New Deal initiatives. Although the modern Social Security program bears little resemblance to that established under the original act, complaints that it undermines self-sufficiency and forces hardworking citizens to pay for the irrationalities of other people are strikingly similar to the objections raised at its inception. In fact, political support for the Social Security Act was not mobilized by a call for altruism or individual sacrifice for the sake of the common good. To the contrary, FDR insisted that the program be structured in such a way that Social Security taxes were directly connected with benefits. Thus the average citizen believed that he was in fact saving for his own retirement, not for that of others. Social Security therefore was not conceived, or was it promoted, as a relief program or a large-scale government charity. With regard to the debate over whether or not the system should be contributory, FDR revealed a keen insight into the American character:

> But those taxes were never a problem of economics. They are politics all the way through. We put those payroll contributions there so as to give the contributors a legal, moral, and political right to collect their pensions and their unemployment benefits. With those taxes in there, no damn politician can ever scrap my social security program.[59]

Similarly, the Federal Deposit Insurance Corporation (FDIC) tapped self-interest in order to restore confidence in the private banking system. Despite considerable support for a federal takeover, Roosevelt sought to reform, rather than fundamentally change, the traditional role of private banking in the American economy. By insuring individuals' deposits, the FDIC strongly communicated FDR's strategy of support for the banking establishment. Federal regulation and FDIC standards for member banks, under existing conditions, visibly served the interests of the banking community as well as those of depositors. Overall, the FDIC did much to restore confidence in the system and to rebuild the linkages among bankers, depositors, and creditors so important to the long-term interests of the nation.[60]

It is at least reasonable to suggest that one of the principal reasons why the Social Security and the FDIC programs succeeded was their capacity to make self-interested participation the engine of administrative arrangements that served the general or public good. Along these lines, it is also interesting to note that both programs (and their administrators) have enjoyed a relatively high degree of public support and confidence. It is likely that Social Security's present political difficulties are related to the growing visibility of its redistributive activities—activities translating into taxes for programs that average contributors do not see as being clearly connected to their personal welfare.[61]

Guideline 4: Applying Tocqueville's precepts, design relief programs that promote independence and self-respect. A hallmark of the New Deal was its use of relief programs involving public service jobs. Previously, public relief had applied degrading means tests and cash payments (the dole) to people ruled eligible. Many who were eligible and in desperate need of help refused to apply under these conditions. The Works Progress Administration (WPA) and the Civilian Conservation Corps (CCC) are a couple of examples of FDR's opposition to direct relief, a position he took because he believed that the dole crushed self-respect and in the long term increased hostility toward government.[62] The Public Works Administration (PWA), the Home Owner's Loan Corporation (HOLC), and the greatly expanded use of the Reconstruction Finance Corporation (RFC) represent a variety of programs intended to bolster a wide range of middle-class interests without disturbing this group's sense of self-reliance and its confidence in American political institutions.[63]

STATESMANSHIP AND PUBLIC ADMINISTRATION

The evaluative literature on Franklin Roosevelt and the New Deal tends to characterize both as operating without anything approaching a conceptually consistent strategy for confronting the economic and political problems arising from the depression. Expert commentators still debate the economic impact of the New Deal.[64] Yet the New Deal is politically instructive because it demonstrates how public administration may be used in ways that are both positive and congruent with the understanding of the American character that guided the Founders. In these terms, Roosevelt acted in a manner designed to broaden substantially and permanently our understanding of the role of the state and its administrative arm in American society. Herbert Storing captures the nature of FDR's statesmanship:

> There may be needed, however, rarely but occasionally, what might be called *high American statesmanship,* or high liberal statesmanship, comparable to that of the Founders themselves. The requirements here are an extraordinary (and perhaps ultimately inexplicable) devotion to public duty and an understanding of the principles of governmental structure and operation of the broadest and deepest kind. Note that this statesmanship is still, in a fundamental sense, "administrative."[65]

The public service in America is now being severely tested. The character of this challenge is quite different from that confronted by government in 1932, but in at least two ways, the problem is similar. First, the place of public administration in the American regime is being questioned, and a major effort to redefine its role is taking place. Second, much of the controversy surrounding public administration is concerned with its effect on the character of the citizenry. The preceding guidelines are an attempt to show how those leaders who thoroughly understand the relationships among democracy, administration, and character may be able to translate them into policies firmly grounded in Founding principles.

7

Administrative Ethics
and Founding Thought

The ancient Greek understanding of *ethos* meant, quite literally, that a group of citizens possessed a distinctive set of traits that constituted their character. A principal function of the *polis* (a term that encompassed far more than our contemporary *state* or *government* and is imperfectly rendered by our word *regime*) was to nurture or inculcate the distinctive traits that it valued—say, a love of honor, wealth, moderation, political courage—into the citizenry. Carried out consistently and successfully throughout the regime, this practice produced a recognizable character-type who personified the way of life of that particular people. According to Aristotle, this nurturing could occur successfully only within the *polis* or regime, and the very best of these regimes attempted to promote the highest possible character, that which pursued the "advantageous and just" while avoiding the "harmful and unjust."[1] Indeed, the nurturing of these traits was most decidedly a political act, one that decisively linked ethics and politics. (This linkage was reflected in the very titles of Aristotle's two great works, *Nicomachean Ethics* and *Politics*.[2])

Even if one's regime was imperfect and so did not pursue the highest of these ideal traits, the inculcation of the desired character was still no easy accomplishment. Not only did the regime have to agree on the way of life it wanted for the citizenry, but it also then had to try mightily to foster the traits in ways both large and small. (Our contemporary distinction between the public and private spheres would have little place here.) In addition to requiring a far more expansive understanding of morality than we now have,[3] this effort also necessitated an agreement on what happiness or the good life was, for reaching (or living) it was the ultimate reason one was attempting to acquire the appropriate character.

This classical understanding of the linkage between ethics and politics was known to the Founders, but by then it was also accompanied by a long history of less than impressive attempts to achieve happiness. Indeed, one could argue that the attempts to achieve it had, in many instances, resulted in the utmost unhappiness for large numbers of people. In the opinion of some thoughtful observers, one reason for the unhappiness was that organized religions competed with philosophy in offering different versions of earthly happiness. With an all-too-predictable frequency, the concerns of the other world seemed to become enmeshed with those of this world. In its most distressing forms, this entanglement meant that the battles between religions over whose idea of happiness should prevail were being waged for them by the regimes they had come to dominate.

This perception that competing ideas about the good life were the cause of so much earthly unhappiness led the Founders to seek alternatives—ones that, in a sense, would deemphasize the Aristotelian linkage between ethics and politics. One of the most persuasive and influential presentations of this view occurs in the first document of our Founding, the Declaration of Independence. Thomas Jefferson, drawing heavily on the work of John Locke, discusses the four "self-evident . . . truths" that form the foundation of man's earthly life. The second of these ("that men are endowed by their Creator with certain unalienable rights"), in addition to acknowledging the important link to the Divine, also includes as illustrative examples "Life, Liberty, and the pursuit of Happiness." By promising mankind that it had an "unalienable right" not to happiness but only to its pursuit, Jefferson implicitly drew attention to at least two important points.

The first of these amounts to a deliberate confession of ignorance by the Founders as to what, precisely, is likely to make mankind happy. Considering the accumulated examples of unhappiness provided by history, it was deemed more prudent to eschew designating a (quite possibly) flawed path to earthly happiness in favor of permitting the citizens a wider range of choices. The key provision, then, is the word *pursuit,* which suggests quite literally that many (if not most) of the citizens in a regime founded in this way may never achieve happiness. (Unless, of course, they take as an acceptable substitute a delight in always pursuing but never achieving the goal of happiness.)

The second point is that a regime founded on what I am calling a confession of ignorance regarding happiness is most unlikely to have a distinctive way of life in the sense originally meant by Aristotle. Although a regime of this kind may come to an agreement about ideas of happiness that should not be promoted within its boundaries (such as those requiring the enslavement of other human beings), it will be much more ambivalent about those that should be permitted. In short, it is far more likely to find itself host to innumerable lifestyles than to a definable way of life. It is possible that such lifestyles will radiate from a general consensus on some core character traits deemed necessary to the regime's survival (such as a love of equality), but it is certain that at least one trait will have to be promoted: a tolerance for the different opinions, beliefs, and actions of one's fellow citizens. (Stated more starkly, a regime with numerous dissimilar lifestyles may have an interest in trying to ensure that citizens are not too passionately attached to their political opinions and religious beliefs, for such attachments impede the development of the requisite level of tolerance.)

DISINTERESTED OR SELF-INTERESTED GOVERNORS?

The Founders of the U.S. Constitution were decidedly ambivalent about the extent to which this contemplated regime of multiple lifestyles would reliably produce a sufficient number of disinterested governors. They hoped that an appropriate number of virtuous public servants would hold elective and appointive posts, but they were far from confident that the American regime would be able to support a classical republic (or confederation of republics) requiring widespread public virtue. In 1787, the pursuit of self-interest seemed more the American norm.[4] This aspect of their thinking is reflected in a Constitution that diffuses and limits governmental powers and frustrates the tyrannical propensities of factions. These precautions, however, do not fully express the Founders' aspirations, for they also expected that the Constitution would "obtain" a fair number of public servants who "possess[ed] most wisdom to discern, and most virtue to pursue, the common good of the society."[5]

Nevertheless, the Founders were realists on this question. They fully expected that selfish "knaves" and "hypocrites" would not be strangers to public office at all levels of American government.[6] A glance back through the past 200-plus years of our national history certainly proves that their fears about such officeholders were not entirely misplaced. However, throughout this history the American regime has also produced many public-spirited men and women who have served the Republic competently and faithfully. Indeed, these seemingly contradictory results only serve to confirm the wisdom of the Founders' level-headed approach to the task of writing a constitution for the American Republic.

The Federalist Papers provides considerable evidence to support the contention that public administration was of great concern to many of the Founders, most notably James Madison and Alexander Hamilton. As John Rohr points out, "If you look at the Federalist papers as an authoritative commentary on the Constitution, the word administration or its cognates are used 124 times. This is more than the words Congress, president, and Supreme Court appear."[7] The written record also strongly suggests that the Founders did not think politics could or should be separate from administration. For example, in *Federalist* No. 72 Publius explains,

The administration of government, in its largest sense, comprehends all the operations of the body politic, whether legislative, executive, or judiciary; but in its most usual and perhaps in its most precise signification, it is limited to executive details, and falls peculiarly within the province of the executive department.[8]

Elsewhere in No. 72 and in other essays of *The Federalist Papers,* Publius makes it quite clear that the purposes of republican government, factional politics, and the separation of powers make it impossible to remove (politicized) executive details from the realm of administration in "its largest sense."[9]

Contemporary efforts to separate administration from politics in the study of public administration prompted one observer to note that an important consequence was to remove questions of character and ethics from the mainstream of the field. In Robert Miewald's words, treating public administrators "as a special class in society not affected by ordinary human weaknesses produced a doctrine that effectively removed the bureaucrat from scholarly scrutiny."[10] If the Founders' understanding of public administration as a political enterprise is accepted, however, questions regarding the character of public administrators cannot easily be treated as secondary issues.[11] As I have argued, this perspective does not permit public administrators to escape the general analyses of representation and of the character of representatives offered by the Founders.

THE CHARACTER OF
THE AMERICAN PUBLIC ADMINISTRATOR

The relevance of Founding thought to matters of administrative conduct, morality, and ethics has surfaced as part of a more general concern with public administration's role in contemporary American society. The commentary in this area contains two general emphases, each of which draws upon key aspects of the

Founders' perspective on public service in the American regime. Their willingness to contemplate a regime in which individual self-interest was accepted as a dominant motive has led some observers to conclude that the Founders intended to rely primarily on constitutional and other mechanisms for channeling and checking self-interest (including that of public administrators). In its purest form, this approach requires no special or elevated character traits of public officials; they need only be like everybody else—predictably self-interested and capable of being moderate and self-restrained.[12]

Other scholars favor an interpretation that stresses the Founders' hope that their constitutional system would encourage the emergence of a "natural aristocracy" of educated and virtuous citizens dedicated to public service and to the preservation of the Republic.[13] Gordon Wood observes that the Federalists in particular "anticipated that somehow the new government would be staffed largely by 'the worthy,' the natural social aristocracy of the country."[14] From this perspective, it is reasonable to expect that public administrators will be disinterested, honorable, and competent servants of the public interest.

Both of these positions find support in the writings of the Founders and in the analyses of those scholars who have studied the intellectual and political wellsprings of Founding thought. The line of reasoning to be examined first has its roots in the Founders' belief that the regime they sought to establish would encourage the development of a disinterested and virtuous "natural aristocracy" of governors. I will then explore the implications for public administration of the Founders' intention to create "a republic which did not require a virtuous people for its sustenance."[15]

The Disinterested Administrator

Do American public administrators have to be exceptionally virtuous in order to carry out the political functions the Founders apparently intended for them? Such a view would unequivocally point to governors who would be truly disinterested men and women capable of rising above private interest in order to identify and advance the common good. Indeed, many of the Founders were far from opposed to the cultivation of such an ideal among an elite of political leaders. James MacGregor Burns characterizes their aspirations:

> They wanted *virtue* in both leaders and citizens. By virtue they meant at the least good character and civic concern; at the most . . . a heroic love for the public good, a devotion to justice, a willingness to sacrifice comfort and riches for the public weal, an elevation of the soul. One reason the Framers believed in representation was that it would refine leadership, acting as a kind of sieve that would separate and elevate the more virtuous elements.[16]

The Founders were raised in a tradition of social and political leadership. Consequently, they saw government as an instrument for moral improvement, not simply as an institutional mechanism for articulating and compromising on a broad spectrum of private interests. Madison, for example, was not a "pluralist" in the contemporary sense of that term. One of the reasons he wanted to see the clashing interests or factions neutralize each other was to permit virtuous men to step in and promote the public good—to act as disinterested umpires in disputes between interests.[17] As a group, the Founders saw leadership or statesmanship as an exceptional quality of "disinterestedness"—of not being influenced by considerations of private gain. "Virtue or disinterestedness, like the concept of honor, lay at the heart of all prescriptions for political leadership in the eighteenth century Anglo-American world."[18] Thus, it seems a fair representation to say that the Founders of the American regime would have treasured public administrators who displayed the appropriate traits that accompany disinterested leadership.

> The Founders . . . passed on ideals and standards of political behavior that helped to contain and control the unruly materialistic passions unleashed by the democratic revolution of the early nineteenth century. Even today our aversion to corruption, our uneasiness over the too blatant promotion of special

interests, and our yearning for examples of unselfish public service suggest that such ideals still have great moral power.[19]

These ideals and standards have become central to much of the contemporary discussion of administrative ethics and morality. The highest standards of conduct and an ability to reason in ethical and moral terms are often asked of the individual public administrator. For example, in his argument for an American Society for Public Administration (ASPA) code of ethics, Ralph Clark Chandler observes that "the real decisions of public officials frequently involve ethical choices and the resolution of ethical dilemmas. . . . An enhanced and self-consciously developed capacity to engage in moral reasoning, and even an occasional glance at a modern version of the Athenian Oath, might help."[20] Similarly, David K. Hart has asserted:

> Public administrators are obligated to serve the first principles upon which the Republic was founded. . . . This means that all those in the public service, whether through election or employment, must be completely . . . committed to those regime values. All public administrators must be moral philosophers and all public administration education must begin with the consideration of regime values.[21]

A related theme takes the form of an obligation to assume a leading role in enhancing the quality of citizenship in our democratic republic. John Rohr summarizes this prescription:

> I would urge the career civil servant to come to terms with his or her role as a part of a governing elite; [and] . . . let the career civil servant work at broadening the base of the elite by encouraging as many of the public as possible to become citizens in the classical mold. . . . The task of the administrator is to invite the participant whose primary concern is quite properly his or her own interest to the higher ground of public interest.[22]

Similarly, Hart points to what he believes is a profound "disaffec-tion" among citizens and public servants, and he attributes it to a loss of "idealism" in the public service.

> In American democracy, *the primary motivation for public service must be a profound commitment to the founding val-ues of our inception, which includes an extensive and active love of others.* That commitment must be reflected in morally appropriate policies, programs, and behaviors, as they relate to the general public, to specific constituent clients, and to col-leagues as well.[23]

Although certainly not meeting with general acceptance in the cur-rent political climate, these and similar expressions concerning the conduct and character of public administrators are not really at odds with the Founders' belief that the American regime would be capable of producing its fair share of virtuous and honorable leaders.[24] More-over, such calls for disinterestedness, nobility, and public-spirited-ness clearly require that public administrators be held to standards far higher than those applied to the average (self-interested) citizen. They embody, therefore, a modern version of the Founders' hope that a properly constituted democratic republic might encourage the emergence of a virtuous governing class. The problem, then as now, is that there is unlikely to be a sufficient number of such governors for the needs of the regime. Indeed, when one contemplates the numerous ways in which intelligent, talented men and women of vir-tuous dispositions are lured away from public service (and into occu-pations such as business, law, or medicine that offer more of the material rewards valued by the regime), it is easy to become gravely concerned about the availability of such individuals for governance.

The Self-interested Administrator

There is compelling evidence that the Founders hoped virtuous, pub-lic-spirited citizens would gravitate to the governance of the regime, yet there is equally strong evidence to support the conclusion that the Founders never intended to base the American regime on the virtue of its citizens and administrators. Their writings, and those of serious students of the Founding period, reveal profound reservations about the extent to which Americans could be expected to rise above self-interest and the inevitability of various factions trying to dominate others. Indeed, Publius is quite explicit on this point: an individual's naturally selfish passions and interests usually can be relied upon to be stronger than the attraction exerted by public ones. In other words, "Publius was too 'realistic' to believe that each citizen was moved by the idea that it would be in his true interest to do what is in the true interest of the nation."[25] Ralph Lerner describes a group of such realists:

> These were no garden-variety eighteenth century ideologues flattering themselves they had an option to create a utopia. Knowing that they could neither stop history nor command it, these Founders turned their thoughts to identifying sources of danger without fancying that they might overcome those dangers once and for all.[26]

The turbulent years under the Articles of Confederation had provided many reasons to doubt that the American Republic could be based on widespread civic virtue. Among the Founders there was a pervasive disappointment with the results of the postrevolutionary experiment in highly democratic, legislatively dominated state governments. Throughout the Confederation, the pursuit of self-interest was the norm, and many observers were quick to identify a potentially fatal mismatch between the optimistic assumptions regarding citizen character that underpinned the new American "republics" and the reality that had emerged since 1776. The Founders "had learned that it was foolish to expect most people to sacrifice their private interests for the sake of the public welfare."[27] Cecilia Kenyon's description of their point of view provides no reason to believe that the Founders were at all inclined to exclude public administrators from this general observation:

[They] shared a profound distrust of man's capacity to use power wisely and well. They believed self-interest to be the dominant motive of political behavior, no matter whether the form of government be republican or monarchical, and they believed in the necessity of constructing political machinery that would restrict the operation of self-interest and prevent men entrusted with political power from abusing it. This was the fundamental assumption of the men who wrote the Constitution, and of those who opposed its adoption, as well.[28]

These are not the views of men who thought public administrators could be relied upon to be disinterested guardians of higher virtues and the common welfare.[29] To the contrary: the Founders were intent on establishing a regime based, as Hamilton said, on human nature as it *was,* not as they might *wish* it to be.[30] This low but solid foundation allowed them to envision a regime that would require very little active supervision by administrative guardians "fitted to perform the function of ruling."[31]

The Founders' refusal to rely on the presence of either citizen virtue or disinterested officeholders is reflected in the literature of public administration, much of which deals with ways of controlling administrative power and ensuring that it is responsive to democratic processes. Administrative and bureaucratic theories, for instance, tend to focus on issues of hierarchy and authority, accountability and responsibility, and political and management-control systems. There also has been continuing attention to public administration's place in the constitutional separation of powers. Statutory, structural, and procedural checks on the exercise of executive power and administrative discretion are enduring topics. Judicial review, legislative oversight, open administrative rulemaking procedures, and merit-based personnel systems routinely are evaluated as restraints on the self-interested ambitions and factional biases of administrators. Each of these concerns, in its own way, is an admission that Publius was correct in his assertion that in framing a government which is to be administered by men over men, the great difficulty lies in this: you must first enable the government to control the governed; and in the next place oblige it to control itself. A dependence on the people is, no doubt, the primary control on the government; but experience has taught mankind the necessity of *auxiliary precautions.*[32]

The development of codes of ethics for public employees ranks among the numerous "auxiliary precautions" scattered throughout our regime. At least by implication, such codes accept Publius's view that men are not angels. In essence, codes such as the one set forth by ASPA are based on the premise that public servants should be held accountable to a set of objective values or standards of conduct. Moral relativism and autonomy are rejected in favor of an external authority—the code of ethics and the reasoning behind it—that substitutes for a potential lack of reliable internal virtues.

According to Ralph Chandler, codes of ethics serve two primary functions, both of which may be seen as falling within this category of "auxiliary precautions." First, they provide specific criteria for judging conduct and, when violations occur, establish grounds for disciplinary action. Second, they are guides for behaviors and choices that are intended to help the individual better serve the common good. From the perspective of these codes, *doing good* does not require that one *be good.*

We do good acts because they have been prescribed by the requirements of virtue, good manners, the revealed word of God, tradition, the elders, the common law, the Constitution, or some other source of transcendent authority; and in the process of doing good acts, we become good.[33]

To the extent that constitutional, organizational, legal, political, professional, and other external ways of improving the chances that public servants will act in a manner that promotes the public interest have stayed on its agenda, American public administration has responded appropriately to the Founders' concerns. It has taken as its starting point a largely unsentimental perspective on the character of the American public administrator. Although they may have preferred governance by the truly disinterested, the Founders thought it prudent to act as if self-interest would be the rule. And there is no sound reason to suppose that they would not apply the same perspective to the greatly enhanced governing role now granted to contemporary public administrators.

ADMINISTRATIVE CHARACTER AND THE AMERICAN REGIME

What, then, do the Founders have to teach us about the ethical foundations of public administration in the American regime? On the one hand, they seem to be saying that a "natural aristocracy" of talent and virtue should be cultivated and that, at least by implication, public administrators should be important members of that group. On the other hand, they are adamant in their insistence on a regime that—once established—should not require for its maintenance anything approaching this elevated standard. Is the current situation one that the Founders would have judged acceptable, perhaps even commendable? One particularly eloquent answer is provided by Alexis de Tocqueville, the influential commentator of the 1830s who so thoroughly evaluated the results of the system that the Founders had established some two generations earlier. His discussion of the American "doctrine of self-interest properly understood" described the ways in which selfish behavior could be turned to public advantage.[34] Similarly, his characterization of rule by the virtuous elites of the era pointed to reasons why such rule was both limited to a relative few and potentially in tension with the mores of a democratic republic.

> When the world was under the control of a few rich and powerful men, they liked to entertain a sublime conception of the duties of man. It gratified them to make out that it is a glorious thing to forget oneself and that one should do good without

self-interest, as God himself does. That was the official doctrine of morality at the time.[35]

The Founders' Constitution establishes a regime that, in important respects, is designed to preclude rule by a few "rich and powerful men." To the degree that "sublime" duties and elevated standards of disinterestedness are associated with rule by aristocratic elites who are not selected by democratic means and disciplined by public opinion, then requiring such virtues of those individuals who govern threatens the moral basis of the American regime. In other words, if nondemocratic means are required to nurture the appropriate virtues of disinterestedness among the most likely leaders of the democratic republic, a formula for continual tension between the rulers and the ruled is built into the regime.[36]

The apparently contradictory nature of the Founders' thought on this issue may be resolved if it is understood that they sought to establish conditions under which disinterested or morally elevated administration could emerge, but not at the expense of republican government, democratic values, or the realistic definition of human nature that underpins the Constitution. Martin Diamond addresses this point in his critique of Richard Hofstadter's argument that the Founders' idea of human nature should be revised along "humanistic" lines, thereby allowing the establishment of a more ennobling political system.

Hofstadter's entire criticism of the American Founding rests upon his apparent certainty that it is going to be possible "to change the nature of man to conform with a more ideal system." . . . He seems to take from the Aristotelian enterprise something of the elevation to which virtue is thought capable of reaching but strips it of its corollary severity and inegalitarianism; and this "high toned" expectation regarding virtue he apparently combines with the democracy and commodious well-being of Madison's enterprise, but strips it of *its* corollary, the foundation in the system of opposite and rival interests. Such complacent synthesizing or combining of irreconcilables is the hallmark of contemporary utopianism.[37]

For American public administration, the implications are clear: whatever excellences of character are asked of the administrator—or asked by the administrator of the citizens—must be derived from ones that are firmly rooted in the regime's foundation. Clearly, some of the Founders were optimistic that a natural aristocracy would be "obtained" within the framework of the Constitution. (Thomas Jefferson is particularly well known for his belief that an aristocracy of merit could be developed and that Americans would freely consent to be governed by such individuals.) However, their concept of democratic republicanism "never denied the unequal existence of human virtues or excellences; it only denied the ancient claim of excellence to *rule as a matter of right.*"[38] In the American regime, moral and intellectual excellence—the true foundations of a natural aristocracy—could rule only through popular consent and only in conformance with constitutional requisites.

Thus, remaining within the Founders' framework requires that any effort to elevate administrative character above the minimal level needed to sustain the Republic be balanced fully by a concern with "effectual precautions for keeping [administrators] virtuous while they continue to hold their public trust." The most effectual precaution, of course, is to assume that people are self-interested and moved by a variety of motives, only some of which are likely to be realized through serving the public good.[39] At a minimum, the Founders' perspective instructs us not to exclude public administrators from this assumption.

POLITICS, ADMINISTRATION, AND REGIME PRINCIPLES

The Founders insisted that the survival of the Republic not be dependent on a highly virtuous citizenry led by disinterested governors. They were optimistic that the United States would produce

its fair share of virtuous citizens and leaders, but character formation was left largely to the workings of institutional arrangements,
representative democracy, and the private realms of family, school,
and community. In the final analysis, the Constitution was intended
to be both an elevating device and a means of ensuring that all people who seek to govern—including public administrators—must
do so with the backing of popular consent, no matter how virtuous
or benevolent they might be.

Woodrow Wilson's "Study of Administration," considered by
some to be the founding document of a self-aware examination of
public administration, is characterized by a series of essentially
irreconcilable statements about the separability of politics and
administration.[40] Though Wilson later disavowed a politics-administration dichotomy, the field in certain respects is still grappling
with a fundamental issue he raised in 1887: how can the study of
public administration be removed from the study of politics and
constitutions without producing a science that is reduced to dealing with structural questions and dangerously disconnected from
the foundations of the regime?[41]

The authors of the Constitution made no such separation. Current treatments of administrative ethics and character that do, either
explicitly or implicitly, are at risk of being trivial or of blindly
undermining the Founders' accomplishments. The Founders' clear-
eyed refusal to split politics from administration denies that public
administrators should be shielded from the assumptions and requirements of the constitutional design and, at the same time, establishes
a productive framework for the study of administrative ethics in
America. Using Wilson's language, from the Founding perspective
the Constitution and the regime it frames are not gases to be distilled
from questions of administrative character. Quite to the contrary,
they must be "touchstones" for meaningful inquiry into this vital
area. Otherwise, we will continually be at risk of "blindly bor-
row[ing] something incompatible with our principles."[42]

8
Epilogue

If Vice-President Al Gore's hearty embrace of "reinventing government" had left any doubts about the durability of the inherent tension between democracy and administration as a political issue, the 1994 midterm elections thoroughly erased them. The Republican congressional majority that subsequently assumed power embarked on a concerted effort to cut the national government's budget and drastically reduce the scope of its powers. If even a portion of that heady congressional rhetoric eventually becomes embodied in law, major federal agencies such as the IRS, Housing and Urban Development (HUD), Commerce, and the Environmental Protection Agency (EPA) seem slated for significant alterations. Some of their functions may well be eliminated, consolidated, or shifted to established state entities. (For example, one proposal to establish a 16 percent national sales tax envisions abolishing the IRS with its 115,000 employees and shifting the tax collection responsibilities to the present retail sales tax apparatus of the states.) Other functions may be modified or shifted in ways that make them more the responsibilities of the ordinary citizen than has previously been the case. (Thus, the National Educational Standards project initiated by the Bush administration now appears to be inconsequential and is probably all but dead. In various states, however, efforts continue apace to place responsibility for "the what and the how" of citizen education more directly in the hands of parents and local communities. The most populist and controversial of these reform efforts envision the use of various types of vouchers as devices for circumventing the power of the professional public school establishment. At least partly in response, educational groups such as the National Education Association [NEA] have begun to back less dramatic reforms—including charter schools.[1])

THE CHALLENGE OF FEDERALISM: CENTRALIZATION VS. DECENTRALIZATION

Prior to the Congress of 1994 and its Contract with America, the United States had witnessed three other major alterations of the original relationship between the national government and the states. The first of these occurred as a result of another powerful Republican Congress that dominated the immediate post–Civil War era. The Radical Republicans of this Reconstruction Congress disdained the moderate policies that Lincoln had hoped would make the reconciliation between the North and the South as painless as possible. Instead, the Congress overran his weak successor, Samuel Johnson (who ultimately was to escape impeachment by only one Senate vote), and implemented draconian measures designed to punish the defeated Confederacy. A recalcitrant South saw former Confederates barred from voting and the ratification of the Fourteenth Amendment—which greatly enhanced the powers of the national government—made a condition for reentry into the Union. Such harsh treatment of fellow citizens left political, cultural, and emotional scars that persist to this day.

The next great augmentation of the powers of the national government was shepherded by a powerful president rather than by a Congress. The Great Depression and World War II together provided Franklin Delano Roosevelt with the rationale for his efforts to centralize more powers in Washington. Some of the earliest policies and programs established by FDR's New Deal (WPA, CCC, and NRA) have long since expired. Others, such as Social Security and a host of alphabet agencies, have continued (albeit in modified form). One reason for some of the success these policies enjoyed is that they made visible connections between the citizenry's self-interest and the benefits to be received. While believing that the problems facing the nation were overwhelming to individuals, Roosevelt still understood that these citizens had to be directly involved in any solutions. In Arthur Schlesinger's description of one such policy (the Agricultural Adjustment Act), the individual citizens were encouraged to see how their self-interests were tied to the needs of the larger community: "Running their own show within a framework of national policy, they educated themselves in social discipline."[2]

The third great alteration in the relations between the national government and the states was also led by another powerful president, Lyndon Baines Johnson. Fueled by the volatile mixture of Kennedy's assassination, the Vietnam War, the civil rights demonstrations, the baby boom, and the continuation of the great post–World War II economic expansion, the Great Society's legacy was to be especially far-reaching. Landmark pieces of legislation intended to foster greater equality in voting, employment, housing, and health care were extracted from a Democratic Congress. Paradoxically, the ways in which some of these legislative rights ultimately expanded the powers of the national government have now served as rallying points for the efforts of the current Congress to effect reforms. The success enjoyed by one powerful nineteenth-century Congress and two strong twentieth-century presidents in shifting the federal balance of power toward the national government will now be challenged by members of a contemporary Congress who are determined to shift it back toward the states.

In this endeavor the Congress surely owes more to the thought of Friedrich Hayek and his followers than to Woodrow Wilson. The fear that centralized planning and authority ultimately destroys the individualism that is the foundation of democratic republicanism can be found at the core of many of the proposed congressional reforms. It takes little analysis of these same reforms to see that they are fundamentally sympathetic to the criticisms of William G. Scott and Frederick Thayer, who supported the view that administrative theorists had constructed elitist rationalizations designed to legitimate the power of professional managers in both the public and private sectors.[3]

Whether reinvented or just revitalized, the uneasy relationship between administration and democracy that has been evident throughout so much of America's history is going to be revisited once again as part of the congressional effort to redistribute the powers of our federal system. As in Congress, the forces at work certainly will favor democratic principles over such undemocratic ones as hierarchy. How, then, is public administration likely to fare in this changed political environment?

If the congressional reforms are successfully implemented over the next several years (and this is certainly a big if, for legislative success ultimately depends on the outcomes of the 1996 elections and beyond), the alterations in federalism are going to favor the states and localities over the national government. From the Madisonian vantage point of self-interest, this decentralization of power may have important personal consequences for public employees of the national government—most especially for the people working in the departments or agencies that may be targeted for elimination. Moreover, it holds forth the prospect of significant change in the states.

In tandem with the movement to privatize various services and to flatten the layers of administrative hierarchy, the decentralization efforts will seek to shift political power and responsibilities (if not funds) to the state and local levels. In so doing, there probably will be less uniformity of policies and priorities among the various states. Because claims of either political neutrality or professional expertise are no longer guaranteed sources of political legitimacy, decentralized public administrators may well use the quality of their service to the citizens/clients/public as an additional justification for their exercise of certain forms of discretionary political powers. In a political climate favoring populism, administrators may seek to defuse some of the inherent tension between administration and democracy through the greatly expanded use of citizen advisory (or even governing) boards. (For example, facing a newly elected school superintendent intent on decentralizing state control over public education, school districts in Georgia—long adroit at allying themselves with sympathetic parents through such traditional organizations as PTAs—are even now starting to seek more advice from local citizen advisory boards on subjects ranging from book selection to instructional approaches.) From one perspective, this approach even surpasses the fundamental political advantage enjoyed by the public service during the height of the patronage period, for instead of seeking a degree of legitimacy delegated from elected officials, in effect it now bypasses them and goes directly to the source of all Lockean-based political powers: the people.

The combination of decentralization of powers, less uniformity of standards, and increased responsibilities for both administrators and citizens may have some positive effects on the quality of citizenship. If Tocqueville was correct in arguing that self-interested American democrats learn their citizens' duties and obligations most thoroughly by interacting (even clashing) with local officials, this arrangement promises to provide instruction on a large scale. From the citizens' perspective, this interaction will require mastering the skills of democracy so that, for example, a proposed public project (be it a roadway, waste-water treatment plant, or school bond referendum) might be effectively countered or supported by a decisive display of numbers. As Tocqueville emphasized, the efforts of individuals are "often less successful" than those of the authorities, but the overall result of "individual strivings amounts to much more than any administration could undertake."[4] This outcome is especially so in regard to the beneficial effects these efforts have on citizen character.

In short, the Madisonian project of moderating factional politics by fostering the proliferation of factions or interest groups is likely to be intensified. Depending on the kinds of passions raised by any given issue, groups will arise, be countered by opponents, and probably die out with the resolution of the animating issue. (For example, a road project that brings out the neighbors in force will either be killed or get built in some form. In either case, the issue is closed as a rallying point for the original factions.) However, the all-important character of the American citizenry will have ample opportunities to assert itself. Under the best conditions, the increased need to associate for public purposes facilitates the transition from self-interested private individual to a more community-oriented citizen.

PUBLIC POLICIES FOR DEMOCRATIC CITIZENS

Decentralization being the case, what kinds of public policies are most likely to be successful? There is no great mystery here. The kinds of policies that traditionally have had the greatest public support (understood as the highest levels of voluntary compliance) are those that visibly and directly tap into the vein of self-interest and channel it toward Tocqueville's "self-interest properly understood." Thus, the authoritarian elements inherent in military conscription have never met with long-term favor in America. Yet transform involuntary conscription into an All-Volunteer Force that competes with colleges and industry for the young and a public policy compatible with the American character emerges.

Similarly, there is substantial agreement that features of our public health-care system need reform. Although legislation has now increased the portability of benefits, solutions are still being sought for reform of coverage for catastrophic illnesses. However, one interesting pilot program was included in the recent health insurance bill that has clear Madisonian overtones. According to its provisions, the tax code will be employed to test the feasibility of certain Medical Savings Accounts (MSAs) to be marketed by private insurance companies. These companies collectively will be able to offer no more than 750,000 policies annually to individuals who are self-employed, uninsured, or who work for companies employing fewer than fifty people. Individuals and employers can make limited tax-deductible contributions to the policyholders'

MSAs. Neither interest on the acounts nor withdrawals to pay medical bills are taxed, and the maximum out-of-pocket expenses incurred by individuals and/or families wuld be limited. The underlying assumption, of course, is that these self-interested policyholders would be vigilant guardians of their own funds and be most attentive to the costs of any medical services they purchased. Of course, these and other proposed policies may not produce the world's best soldiers or ensure the best quality medical care. Still, they are more compatible with the American character and require far less direct administrative superintendence than their predecessors. Lured by high quality technical training, decent wages, a high level of risk assumption, patriotism, or some combination of the four, young citizens volunteer to defend the rest of us from our external enemies. Motivated by self-interest, reasonably healthy Medical Savings Account members presumably would seek out only necessary care and then scrutinize all resulting bills with a skeptical eye. In classic Madisonian fashion, the self-interest of the patient would be used to counter the self-interest of the health care providers by minimizing the opportunities for overcharges as well as for outright fraud.

DEMOCRATIC ADMINISTRATION

If the citizenry may gain enhanced independence, responsibilities, and economic benefits under such arrangements, what do the proposed changes portend for public administrators? In many instances, some observers contend that the redirection of power from Washington could be the catalyst for similar redistributions of power on the state level. Seeking to foster economy and service, the combination of decentralization and flattened hierarchies may enhance administrative discretion at the local level. If the citizens are then more directly involved in some of the ways already suggested (e.g., advisory and governing boards), public administrators will find themselves joining the Tocquevillian project of enhancing the skills of citizenship—and, in many cases, it may be their own skills that are embellished. The ability to organize both internal and external support, a carefully honed understanding of the true needs of the community, and the ability to communicate well at all levels may be far more prized skills than those that are customarily associated with hierarchical administrative approaches that stress the need to educate and "propagandize" the citizenry.[5] At a minimum, a public administration that is more uncertain about the bases of its own legitimacy is unlikely to emphasize the separation or distinction between Them (the governed) and Us (the governors).

Along with its many other responsibilities, public administration has long been considered one of those numerous "undemocratic elements" that helped to "check the fundamental popular impulse[s]."[6] Will it continue to do so? A qualified "yes" must be accompanied by some explanation. For one thing, any entity that is commonly disparaged and seen as a "splendid hate object" by the people whose passions it should be tempering is able to perform that function in only the most limited of ways.[7] Thus, restoring a sense of honor and public virtue to the performance of public duties is critical—especially so if we truly expect public administration to serve in any way as a moderating influence on democratic passions.

Asking public administrators to take public opinion as one of their standards for approbation may seem contradictory under these circumstances, but it is not an impossible task. Public administration certainly finds itself in a difficult position. On the one hand, it needs to bolster its political legitimacy by linking itself much more thoroughly to the people, the ultimate source of all democratic political powers. On the other hand, this contemporary need may make it far less able (if ever it really was able) to resist ill-considered democratic impulses.

It is hoped that the acquisition of a thorough grounding in American political and constitutional thought combined with the greater reliance on the good opinions of the public will go a long way toward providing public administrators with the necessary ballast to survive some of the political changes that are being contemplated. On numerous levels, public administration performs necessary and laudable functions within the American regime. Under the best of circumstances, both it and the nation will emerge rejuvenated by the changes resulting from the present intense debate over the issue that so occupied the Founders, that is, what should be the proper distribution of powers between the citizens and the various levels of their federal system of government?

Appendix A
Declaration of Independence

In CONGRESS, July 4, 1776
THE UNANIMOUS DECLARATION of the thirteen
UNITED STATES OF AMERICA

When in the Course of human events, it becomes necessary for one people to dissolve the political bands, which have connected them with another, and to assume among the powers of the earth, the separate and equal station to which the Laws of Nature and of Nature's God entitle them, a decent respect to the opinions of mankind requires that they should declare the causes which impel them to the separation.—We hold these truths to be self-evident, that all men are created equal, that they are endowed by their Creator with certain unalienable Rights, that among these are Life, Liberty and the pursuit of Happiness.—That to secure these rights, Governments are instituted among Men, deriving their just powers from the consent of the governed,—That whenever any Form of Government becomes destructive of these ends, it is the right of the People to alter or to abolish it, and to institute new Government, laying its foundation on such principles and organizing its powers in such form, as to them shall seem most likely to effect their Safety and

Happiness. Prudence, indeed, will dictate that Governments long established should not be changed for light and transient causes; and accordingly all experience hath shewn, that mankind are more disposed to suffer, while evils are sufferable, than to right themselves by abolishing the forms to which they are accustomed. But when a long train of abuses and usurpations, pursuing invariably the same Object evinces a design to reduce them under absolute Despotism, it is their right, it is their duty, to throw off such Government, and to provide new Guards for their future security.—Such has been the patient sufferance of these Colonies; and such is now the necessity which constrains them to alter their former System of Government. The history of the present King of Great Britain is a history of repeated injuries and usurpations, all having in direct object the establishment of an absolute Tyranny over these States. To prove this, let Facts be submitted to a candid world.—He has refused his Assent to Laws, the most wholesome and necessary for the public good.—He has forbidden his Governors to pass Laws of immediate and pressing importance, unless suspended in their operation till his Assent should be obtained; and when so suspended, he has utterly neglected to attend to them.—He has refused to pass other Laws for the accommodation of large districts of people, unless those people would relinquish the right of Representation in the Legislature, a right inestimable to them and formidable to tyrants only.—He has called together legislative bodies at places unusual, uncomfortable, and distant from the depository of their public Records, for the sole purpose of fatiguing them into compliance with his measures.—He has dissolved Representative Houses repeatedly, for opposing with manly firmness his invasions on the rights of the people.—He has refused for a long time, after such dissolutions, to cause others to be elected; whereby the Legislative powers, incapable of Annihilation, have returned to the People at large for their exercise; the State remaining in the meantime exposed to all the dangers of invasion from without, and convulsions within.—He has endeavoured to prevent the population of these States; for that purpose obstructing the Laws for Naturalization of Foreigners; refusing to pass others to encourage their migrations hither, and raising the conditions of new Appropriations of Lands. He has obstructed the Administration of Justice, by refusing his Assent to Laws for establishing Judiciary powers.—He has made Judges dependent on his Will alone, for the tenure of their offices, and the amount and payment of their salaries.—He has erected a multitude of New Offices, and sent hither swarms of Officers to harass our people, and eat out their substance.—He has kept among us, in times of peace, Standing Armies without the Consent of our legislatures.—He has affected to render the Military independent of and superior to the Civil power.—He has combined with others to subject us to a jurisdiction foreign to our constitution, and unacknowledged by our laws; giving his Assent to their Acts of pretended Legislation.—For quartering large bodies of armed troops among us:—For protecting them, by a mock Trial, from punishment for any Murders which they should commit on the Inhabitants of these States:—For cutting off our Trade with all parts of the world:—For imposing Taxes on us without our Consent:—For depriving us in many cases, of the benefits of Trial by Jury:—For transporting us beyond Seas to be tried for pretended offenses:— For abolishing the free System of English Laws in a neighboring Province, establishing therein an Arbitrary government, and enlarging its Boundaries so as to render it at once an example and fit instrument for introducing the same absolute rule into these Colonies:—For taking away our Charters, abolishing our most valuable Laws, and altering fundamentally the Forms of our Governments:—For suspending our own Legislatures, and declaring themselves invested with power to legislate for us in all cases whatsoever.—He has abdicated Government here, by declaring us out of his Protection and waging War against us.—He has plundered our seas, ravaged our Coasts, burnt our towns, and destroyed the lives of our people.—He is at this time transporting large Armies of foreign Mercenaries to compleat the works of death, desolation and tyranny, already begun with circumstances of Cruelty & perfidy, scarcely paralleled in the most barbarous ages, and totally unworthy the Head of a civilized nation.—He has constrained our fellow Citizens taken Captive on the high Seas to bear Arms against their

Country, to become the executioners of their friends and Brethren, or to fall themselves by their hands.—He has excited domestic insurrections amongst us, and has endeavoured to bring on the inhabitants of our frontiers, the merciless Indian Savages, whose known rule of warfare, is an undistinguished destruction of all ages, sexes and conditions. In every stage of these Oppressions We have Petitioned for Redress in the most humble terms: Our repeated Petitions have been answered only by repeated injury. A Prince whose character is thus marked by every act which may define a Tyrant, is unfit to be the ruler of a free people. Nor have We been wanting in attentions to our British brethren. We have warned them from time to time of attempts by their legislature to extend an unwarrantable jurisdiction over us. We have reminded them of the circumstances of our emigration and settlement here. We have appealed to their native justice and magnanimity, and we have conjured them by the ties of our common kindred to disavow these usurpations, which would inevitably interrupt our connections and correspondence. They too have been deaf to the voice of justice and of consanguinity. We must, therefore, acquiesce in the necessity, which denounces our Separation, and hold them, as we hold the rest of mankind, Enemies in War, in Peace Friends.—

We, therefore, the Representatives of the united States of America, in General Congress, Assembled, appealing to the Supreme Judge of the world for the rectitude of our intentions do, in the Name, and by the Authority of the good People of these Colonies, solemnly publish and declare, That these United Colonies are, and of Right ought to be Free and Independent States; that they are Absolved from all Allegiance to the British Crown, and that all political connection between them and the State of Great Britain, is and ought to be totally dissolved; and that as Free and Independent States, they have full Power to levy War, conclude Peace, contract Alliances, establish Commerce, and to do all other Acts and Things which Independent States may of right do.—And for the support of this Declaration, with a firm reliance on the protection of divine Providence, we mutually pledge to each other our Lives, our Fortunes and our sacred Honor.

Appendix B
Federalist No. 10

To the People of the State of New York:

Among the numerous advantages promised by a well-constructed Union, none deserves to be more accurately developed than its tendency to break and control the violence of faction. The friend of popular governments never finds himself so much alarmed for their character and fate as when he contemplates their propensity to this dangerous vice. He will not fail, therefore, to set a due value on any plan which, without violating the principles to which he is attached, provides a proper cure for it. The instability, injustice, and confusion introduced into the public councils, have, in truth, been the mortal diseases under which popular governments have every where perished; as they continue to be the favorite and fruitful topics from which the adversaries to liberty derive their most specious declamations. The valuable improvements made by the American constitutions on the popular models, both ancient and modern, cannot certainly be too much admired; but it would be an unwarrantable partiality to contend that they have as effectually obviated the danger on this side as was wished and expected. Complaints are every where heard from our most considerate and virtuous citizens, equally the friends of public and private faith and of public and personal liberty, that our governments are too unstable, that the public good is disregarded in the conflicts of rival parties, and that measures are too often decided, not according to the rules of justice and the rights of the minor party, but by the superior force of an interested and overbearing majority. However anxiously we may wish that these complaints had no foundation, the evidence of known facts will not permit us to deny that they are in some degree true. It will be found, indeed, on a candid review of our situation, that some of the distresses under which we labor, have been erroneously charged on the operation of our governments; but it will be found, at the same time, that other causes will not alone account for many of our heaviest misfortunes; and particularly, for that prevailing and increasing distrust of public engagements, and alarm for private rights, which are echoed from one end of the continent to the other. These must be chiefly, if not wholly, effects of the unsteadiness and injustice with which a factious spirit has tainted our public administrations.

By a faction I understand a number of citizens, whether amounting to a majority or minority of the whole, who are united and actuated by some common impulse of passion, or of interest, adverse to the rights of other citizens, or to the permanent and aggregate interests of the community.

There are two methods of curing the mischiefs of faction: the one, by removing its causes; the other, by controlling its effects.

There are again two methods of removing the causes of faction: the one, by destroying the liberty which is essential to its existence; the other, by giving to every citizen the same opinions, the same passions, and the same interests.

It could never be more truly said than of the first remedy that it is worse than the disease. Liberty is to faction, what air is to fire, an aliment without which it instantly expires. But it could not be a less folly to abolish liberty, which is essential to political life, because it nourishes faction, than it would be to wish the annihilation of air, which is essential to animal life, because it imparts to fire its destructive agency.

The second expedient is as impracticable as the first would be unwise. As long as the reason of man continues fallible, and he is at liberty to exercise it, different opinions will be formed. As long as the connection subsists between his reason and his self-love, his opinions and his passions will have a reciprocal influence on each other; and the former will be objects to which the latter will attach themselves. The diversity in the faculties of men, from which the rights of property originate, is not less an insuperable obstacle to a uniformity of interests. The protection of these faculties is the first object of Government. From the protection of different and unequal faculties of acquiring property, the possession of different degrees and kinds of property immediately results; and from the influence of these on the sentiments and views of the respective proprietors ensues a division of the society into different interests and parties.

The latent causes of faction are thus sown in the nature of man; and we see them everywhere brought into different degrees of activity, according to the different circumstances of civil society. A zeal for different opinions concerning religion, concerning government, and many other points, as well of speculation as of practice; an attachment to different leaders ambitiously contending for pre-eminence and power; or to persons of other descriptions whose fortunes have been interesting to the human passions, have, in turn, divided mankind into parties, inflamed them with mutual animosity, and rendered them much more disposed to vex and oppress each other than to co-operate for their common good. So strong is this propensity of mankind to fall into mutual animosities that, where no substantial occasion presents itself, the most frivolous and fanciful distinctions have been sufficient to kindle their unfriendly passions and excite their most violent conflicts. But the most common and durable source of factions has been the various and unequal distribution of property. Those who hold and those who are without property have ever formed distinct interests in society. Those who are creditors, and those who are debtors, fall under a like discrimination. A landed interest, a manufacturing interest, a mercantile interest, a monied interest, with many lesser interests, grow up of necessity in civilized nations, and divide them into different classes, actuated by different sentiments and views. The regulation of these various and interfering interests forms the principal task of modern legislation, and involves the spirit of party and faction in the necessary and ordinary operations of government.

No man is allowed to be a judge in his own cause, because his interest would certainly bias his judgment, and, not improbably, corrupt his integrity. With equal, nay with greater reason, a body of men are unfit to be both judges and parties at the same time; yet what are many of the most important acts of legislation but so many judicial determinations, not indeed concerning the rights of single persons, but concerning the rights of large bodies of citizens? And what are the different classes of legislators but advocates and parties to the causes which they determine? Is a law proposed concerning private debts? It is a question to which the creditors are parties on one side, and the debtors on the other. Justice ought to hold the balance between them. Yet the parties are, and must be, themselves the judges; and the most numerous party, or, in other words, the most powerful faction, must be expected to prevail. Shall domestic manufactures be encouraged, and in what degree, by restrictions on foreign manufactures? are questions which would be differently decided by the landed and the manufacturing classes, and probably by neither with a sole regard to justice and the public good. The apportionment of taxes on the various descriptions of property is an act which seems to require the most exact impartiality; yet there is, perhaps, no legislative act in which greater opportunity and temptation are given to a predominant party to trample on the rules of justice. Every shilling with which they overburden the inferior number, is a shilling saved to their own pockets.

It is in vain to say that enlightened statesmen will be able to adjust these clashing interests, and render them all subservient to the public good. Enlightened statesmen will not always be at the helm. Nor, in many cases, can such an adjustment be made at all without taking into view indirect and remote considerations, which will rarely prevail over the immediate interest which one party may find in disregarding the rights of another or the good of the whole.

The inference to which we are brought is that the *causes* of faction cannot be removed, and that relief is only to be sought in the means of controlling its *effects*.

If a faction consists of less than a majority, relief is supplied by the republican principle, which enables the majority to defeat its sinister views by regular vote. It may clog the administration, it may convulse the society; but it will be unable to execute and mask its violence under the forms of the Constitution. When a majority is included in a faction, the form of popular government, on the other hand, enables it to sacrifice to its ruling passion or interest both the public good and the rights of other citizens. To secure the public good and private rights against the danger of such a faction, and at the same time to preserve the spirit and the form of popular government, is then the great object to which our enquiries are directed. Let me add that it is the great desideratum by which alone this form of government can be rescued from the opprobrium under which it has so long labored, and be recommended to the esteem and adoption of mankind.

By what means is this object attainable? Evidently by one of two only. Either the existence of the same passion or interest in a majority at the same time must be prevented, or the majority, having such coexistent passion or interest, must be rendered, by their number and local situation, unable to concert and carry into effect schemes of oppression. If the impulse and the opportunity be suffered to coincide, we well know that neither moral nor religious motives can be relied on as an adequate control. They are not found to be such on the injustice and violence of individuals, and lose their efficacy in proportion to the number combined together, that is, in proportion as their efficacy becomes needful.

From this view of the subject, it may be concluded, that a pure democracy, by which I mean a society consisting of a small number of citizens, who assemble and administer the government in person, can admit of no cure for the mischiefs of faction. A common passion or interest will, in almost every case, be felt by a majority of the whole; a communication and concert results from the form of Government itself; and there is nothing to check the inducements to sacrifice the weaker party or an obnoxious individual. Hence it is that such Democracies have ever been spectacles of turbulence and contention; have ever been found incompatible with personal security or the rights of property; and have in general been as short in their lives as they have been violent in their deaths. Theoretic politicians, who have patronized this species of government, have erroneously supposed that by reducing mankind to a perfect equality in their political rights, they would, at the same time, be perfectly equalized and assimilated in their possessions, their opinions, and their passions.

A republic, by which I mean a government in which the scheme of representation takes place, opens a different prospect and promises the cure for which we are seeking. Let us examine the points in which it varies from pure democracy, and we shall comprehend both the nature of the cure and the efficacy which it must derive from the Union.

The two great points of difference between a democracy and a republic are: first, the delegation of the government, in the latter, to a small number of citizens elected by the rest; secondly, the greater number of citizens, and greater sphere of country, over which the latter may be extended.

The effect of the first difference is, on the one hand, to refine and enlarge the public views by passing them through the medium of a chosen body of citizens, whose wisdom may best discern the true interest of their country, and whose patriotism and love of justice will be least likely to sacrifice it to temporary or partial considerations. Under such a regulation, it may well happen that the public voice, pronounced by the representatives of the people, will be more consonant to the public good than if pronounced by the people themselves, convened for the purpose. On the other hand, the effect may be inverted. Men of factious tempers, of local prejudices, or of sinister designs, may by intrigue, by corruption, or by other means, first obtain the suffrages, and then betray the interests of the people. The question resulting is, whether small or extensive republics are most favorable to the election of proper guardians of the public weal: and it is clearly decided in favor of the latter by two obvious considerations.

In the first place, it is to be remarked that, however small the republic may be, the representatives must be raised to a certain number in order to guard against the cabals of a few; and that, however large it may be, they must be limited to a certain number, in order to guard against the confusion of a multitude. Hence the number of representatives in the two cases, not being in proportion to that of the constituents, and being proportionally greatest in the small republic, it follows that if the proportion of fit characters be not less in the large than in the small republic, the former will present a greater option, and consequently a greater probability of a fit choice.

In the next place, as each representative will be chosen by a greater number of citizens in the large than in the small republic, it will be more difficult for unworthy candidates to practise with success the vicious arts by which elections are too often carried; and the suffrages of the people being more free, will be more likely to center on men who possess the most attractive merit and the most diffusive and established characters.

It must be confessed that in this, as in most other cases, there is a mean, on both sides of which inconveniencies will be found to lie. By enlarging too much the number of electors, you render the representative too little acquainted with all their local circumstances and lesser interests; as by reducing it too much, you render him unduly attached to these, and too little fit to comprehend and pursue great and national objects. The federal Constitution forms a happy combination in this respect; the great and aggregate interests being referred to the national, the local and particular to the State legislatures.

The other point of difference is the greater number of citizens and extent of territory which may be brought within the compass of republican than of democratic government; and it is this circumstance principally which renders factious combinations less to be dreaded in the former than in the latter. The smaller the society, the fewer probably will be the distinct parties and interests composing it; the fewer the distinct parties and interests, the more frequently will a majority be found of the same party; and the smaller the number of individuals composing a majority, and the smaller the compass within which they are placed, the more easily will they concert and execute their plans of oppression. Extend the sphere, and you take in a greater variety of parties and interests; you make it less probable that a majority of the whole will have a common motive to invade the rights of other citizens; or if such a common motive exists, it will be more difficult for all who feel it to discover their own strength and to act in unison with each other. Besides other impediments, it may be remarked that, where there is a consciousness of unjust or dishonorable purposes, communication is always checked by distrust in proportion to the number whose concurrence is necessary.

Hence, it clearly appears, that the same advantage which a republic has over a democracy, in controlling the effects of faction, is enjoyed by a large over a small Republic—is enjoyed by the Union over the States composing it. Does this advantage consist in the substitution of representatives whose enlightened views and virtuous sentiments render them superior to local prejudices and to schemes of injustice? It will not be denied that the representation of the Union will be most likely to possess these requisite endowments. Does it consist in the greater security afforded by a greater variety of parties against the event of any one party being able to outnumber and oppress the rest? In an equal degree does the increased variety of parties comprised within the Union increase this security. Does it, in fine, consist in the greater obstacles opposed to the concert and accomplishment of the secret wishes of an unjust and interested majority? Here, again, the extent of the Union gives it the most palpable advantage.

The influence of factious leaders may kindle a flame within their particular States but will be unable to spread a general conflagration through the other States. A religious sect may degenerate into a political faction in a part of the Confederacy; but the variety of sects dispersed over the entire face of it must secure the national councils against any danger from that source. A rage for paper money, for an abolition of debts, for an equal division of property, or for any other improper or wicked project, will be less apt to pervade the whole body of the Union than a particular member of it, in the same proportion as such a malady is more likely to taint a particular county or district than an entire State.

In the extent and proper structure of the Union, therefore, we behold a republican remedy for the diseases most incident to republican government. And according to the degree of pleasure and pride we feel in being republicans ought to be our zeal in cherishing the spirit and supporting the character of Federalists.

PUBLIUS

Appendix C
Federalist No. 51

To the People of the State of New York:

To what expedient, then, shall we finally resort, for maintaining in practice the necessary partition of power among the several departments as laid down in the Constitution? The only answer that can be given is that as all these exterior provisions are found to be inadequate, the defect must be supplied, by so contriving the interior structure of the government as that its constituent parts may, by their mutual relations, be the means of keeping each other in their proper places. Without presuming to undertake a full development of this important idea, I will hazard a few general observations which may perhaps place it in a clearer light, and enable us to form a more correct judgment of the principles and structure of the government planned by the convention.

In order to lay a due foundation for that separate and distinct exercise of the different powers of government, which to a certain extent is admitted on all hands to be essential to the preservation of liberty, it is evident that each department should have a will of its own; and consequently should be so constituted that the members of each should have as little agency as possible in the appointment of the members of the others. Were this principle rigorously adhered to, it would require that all the appointments for the supreme executive, legislative, and judiciary magistracies should be drawn from the same fountain of authority, the people, through channels having no communication whatever with one another. Perhaps such a plan of constructing the several departments would be less difficult in practice than it may in contemplation appear. Some difficulties, however, and some additional expense would attend the execution of it. Some deviations, therefore, from the principle must be admitted. In the constitution of the judicial department in particular, it might be inexpedient to insist rigorously on the principle: first, because peculiar qualifications being essential in the members, the primary consideration ought to be to select that mode of choice which best secures these qualifications; second, because the permanent tenure by which the appointments are held in that department must soon destroy all sense of dependence on the authority conferring them.

It is equally evident that the members of each department should be as little dependent as possible on those of the others for the emoluments annexed to their offices. Were the executive magistrate, or the judges, not independent of the legislature in this particular, their independence in every other would be merely nominal.

But the great security against a gradual concentration of the several powers in the same department consists in giving to those who administer each department the necessary constitutional means and personal motives to resist encroachments of the others. The provision for defense must in this, as in all other cases, be made commensurate to the danger of attack. Ambition must be made to counteract ambition. The interest of the man must be connected with the constitutional rights of the place. It may be a reflection on human nature that such devices should be necessary to control the abuses of government. But what is government itself but the greatest of all reflections on human nature? If men were angels, no government would be necessary. If angels were to govern men, neither external nor internal controls on government would be necessary. In framing a government which is to be administered by men over men, the great difficulty lies in this: You must first enable the government to control the governed; and in the next place oblige it to control itself. A dependence on the people is, no doubt, the primary control on the government; but experience has taught mankind the necessity of auxiliary precautions.

This policy of supplying by opposite and rival interests, the defect of better motives, might be traced through the whole system of human affairs, private as well as public. We see it particularly displayed in all the subordinate distributions of power, where the constant aim is to divide and arrange the several offices in such a manner as that each may be a check on the other—that the private interest of every individual may be a sentinel over the public rights. These inventions of prudence cannot be less requisite in the distribution of the supreme powers of the State.

But it is not possible to give to each department an equal power of self-defense. In republican government, the legislative authority necessarily predominates. The remedy for this inconveniency is to divide the legislature into different branches; and to render them by different modes of election and different principles of action, as little connected with each other as the nature of their common functions and their common dependence on the society will admit. It may even be necessary to guard against dangerous encroachments by still further precautions. As the weight of the legislative authority requires that it should be thus divided, the weakness of the executive may require, on the other hand, that it should be fortified. An absolute negative on the legislature appears, at first view, to be the natural defense with which the executive magistrate should be armed. But perhaps it would be neither altogether safe nor alone sufficient. On ordinary occasions it might not be exerted with the requisite firmness, and on extraordinary occasions it might be perfidiously abused. May not this defect of an absolute negative be supplied by some qualified connection between this weaker department and the weakest branch of the stronger department, by which the latter may be led to support the constitutional rights of the former, without being too much detached from the rights of its own department?

If the principles on which these observations are founded be just, as I persuade myself they are, and they be applied as a criterion to the several State constitutions, and to the federal Constitution, it will be found that if the latter does not perfectly correspond with them, the former are infinitely less able to bear such a test.

There are, moreover, two considerations particularly applicable to the federal system of America, which place the system in a very interesting point of view.

First. In a single republic, all the power surrendered by the people is submitted to the administration of a single government; and usurpations are guarded against by a division of the government into distinct and separate departments. In the compound republic of America, the power surrendered by the people is first divided between two distinct governments, and then the portion allotted to each subdivided among distinct and separate departments. Hence a double security arises to the rights of the people. The different governments will control each other, at the same time that each will be controlled by itself.

Second. It is of great importance in a republic not only to guard the society against the oppression of its rulers, but to guard one part of the society against the injustice of the other part. Different interests necessarily exist in different classes of citizens. If a majority be united by a common interest, the rights of the minority will be insecure. There are but two methods of providing against this evil: the one by creating a will in the community independent of the majority—that is, of the society itself; the other, by comprehending in the society so many separate descriptions of citizens as will render an unjust combination of a majority of the whole very improbable, if not improbable. The first method prevails in all governments possessing an hereditary or self-appointed authority. This, at best, is but a precarious security; because a power independent of the society may as well espouse the unjust views of the major as the rightful interests of the minor party, and may possibly be turned against both parties. The second method will be exemplified in the federal republic of the United States. Whilst all authority in it will be derived from and dependent on the society, the society itself will be broken into so many parts, interests and classes of citizens, that the rights of individuals or of the minority, will be in little danger from interested combinations of the majority. In a free government the security for civil rights must be the same as for religious rights. It consists in the one case in the multiplicity of interests, and in the other in the multiplicity of sects. The degree of security in both cases will depend on the number of interests and sects; and this may be presumed to depend on the extent of country and number of people comprehended under the same government. This view of the subject must particularly recommend a proper federal system to all the sincere and considerate friends of republican government, since it shews that in exact proportion as the territory of the Union may be formed into more circumscribed confederacies, or States, oppressive combinations of a majority will be facilitated, the best security, under the republican forms, for the rights of every class of citizen, will be diminished; and consequently the stability and independence of some member of the government, the only other security, must be proportionally increased. Justice is the end of government. It is the end of civil society. It ever has been and ever will be pursued until it be obtained, or until liberty be lost in the pursuit. In a society under the forms of which the stronger faction can readily unite and oppress the weaker, anarchy may as truly be said to reign as in a state of nature, where the weaker individual is not secured against the violence of the stronger; and as, in the latter state, even the stronger individuals are prompted, by the uncertainty of their condition, to submit to a government which may protect the weak as well as themselves; so, in the former state, will the more powerful factions or parties be gradually induced, by a like motive, to wish for a government which will protect all parties, the weaker as well as the more powerful. It can be little doubted that if the state of Rhode Island was separated from the confederacy and left to itself, the insecurity of rights under the popular form of government within such narrow limits would be displayed by such reiterated oppressions of factious majorities that some power altogether independent of the people would soon be called for by the voice of the very factions whose misrule had proved the necessity of it. In the extended republic of the United States, and among the great variety of interests, parties, and sects which it embraces, a coalition of a majority of the whole society could seldom take place on any other principles than those of justice and the general good; whilst there being thus less danger to a minor from the will of the major party, there must be less pretext, also, to provide for the security of the former, by introducing into the government a will not dependent on the latter, or, in other words, a will independent of the society itself. It is no less certain than it is important, notwithstanding the contrary opinions which have been entertained, that the larger the society, provided it lie within a practicable sphere, the more duly capable it will be of self-government. And happily for the *republican cause,* the practicable sphere may be carried to a very great extent by a judicious modification and mixture of the *federal principle.*

PUBLIUS

Notes

CHAPTER 1. INTRODUCTION

1. George A. Gallup, *The Gallup Poll, Public Opinion 1935–1971* (New York: Random House, 1972), 1: 12ff.

2. James MacGregor Burns, *Roosevelt: The Lion and the Fox* (New York: Harcourt, Brace and World, 1956).

3. For example, see Milton Friedman, *Capitalism and Freedom* (Chicago: University of Chicago Press, 1962), esp. 2–36, and Thomas Sowell, *Markets and Minorities* (New York: Basic Books, 1981), 103–24.

4. Murray Edelman, *Political Language: Words That Succeed and Policies That Fail* (New York: Academic Press, 1977).

5. For a useful summary, see Charles T. Goodsell, *The Case for Bureaucracy: A Public Administration Polemic* (Chatham, N.J.: Chatham House Publishers, 1983).

6. Friedrich A. Hayek, *The Road to Serfdom* (Chicago: University of Chicago Press, 1944), 13–23, and Adam Smith, *The Wealth of Nations,* ed. Edwin Cannan (New York: G. P. Putnam's Sons, 1904).

7. John Chester Miller, *The Wolf by the Ears: Thomas Jefferson and Slavery* (New York: Free Press, 1977).

8. James Madison's *Federalist* No. 10 provides perhaps the most succinct discussion of the Founders' concern with majority tyranny. By dividing the majority into many small factions moderately animated by economic interests rather than by potentially divisive strong opinions and passions, it was rendered generally incapable of tyrannizing over most

minorities. See Alexander Hamilton, James Madison, and John Jay, *The Federalist Papers,* intro. Clinton Rossiter (New York: New American Library, 1961) (hereafter *Federalist Papers*), Martin Diamond, "Ethics and Politics: The American Way," in *The Moral Foundations of the American Republic,* ed. Robert H. Horwitz, 2d ed. (Charlottesville: University of Virginia Press, 1979); and Alexis de Tocqueville, *Democracy in America,* ed. J. P. Mayer (Garden City, N.Y.: Anchor Books, 1969), esp. 259–61, 262–76, and 435–36.

9. See Goodsell, *Case for Bureaucracy,* esp. 38–60 and 82–109.

10. Max Weber, *Economy and Society,* ed. Guenther Roth and Claus Wittich, 2 vols. (Berkeley: University of California Press, 1978), 2: 1451.

11. See Arthur M. Schlesinger, *The Age of Roosevelt: The Politics of Upheaval* (Boston: Houghton Mifflin, 1960), and William E. Leuchtenburg, *In the Shadow of FDR: From Harry Truman to Ronald Reagan* (Ithaca, N.Y.: Cornell University Press, 1983).

12. See David K. Hart, "The Honorable Bureaucrat Among the Philistines," *Administration and Society,* 15 (May 1983): 43–48; see also John A. Rohr, *Ethics for Bureaucrats* (New York: Dekker, 1978).

13. See Laurence J. O'Toole, Jr., "American Public Administration and the Idea of Reform," *Administration and Society,* 16 (August 1984): 141–66.

14. Dwight Waldo, *The Administrative State* (New York: Ronald Press, 1948).

15. See Paul P. Van Riper, "The American Administrative State: Wilson and the Founders—An Unorthodox View," *Public Administration Review* 43 (November/December 1983): 477–90.

16. For example, see Waldo, *Administrative State.*

17. See Charles H. Levine, "Organizational Decline and Cutback Management," *Public Administration Review* 38 (July/August 1978): 316–25, and Andrew D. Glassberg, "The Urban Fiscal Crisis Becomes Routine," *Public Administration Review* 41 (Special Issue 1981): 165–72. The latest example of corporate inquiries into government practices, of course, is the Grace Commission. See Charles T. Goodsell, "The Grace Commission: Seeking Efficiency for the Whole People?" *Public Administration Review* 44 (May/June 1984): 196–204.

18. See Susan J. Tolchin and Martin Tolchin, *Dismantling America: The Rush to Deregulate* (Boston: Houghton Mifflin, 1983); George Gilder, *Wealth and Poverty* (New York: Basic Books, 1981); and Milton Friedman and Rose Friedman, *Tyranny of the Status Quo* (San Diego, Calif.: Harcourt Brace Jovanovich, 1984).

19. This is a majority made up of overlapping interest groups.

20. Arthur M. Schlesinger, Jr., *The Age of Roosevelt: The Crisis of the Old Order, 1919–1933* (Boston: Houghton Mifflin, 1957).

21. See Carl J. Friedrich, *An Introduction to Political Theory* (New York: Harper and Row, 1967), 4–5.

22. U.S. Department of Commerce, Bureau of the Census, *Historical Statistics of the United States: Colonial Times to 1970* (Washington, D.C.: U.S. Government Printing Office, 1975).

23. Ibid.

24. In the United States, strong national government has not resulted in constrained civil liberties; actually, the federal government has often taken the lead in expanding and protecting them, such as in the various statutes enacted during the past two decades to protect voting, housing, and employment rights.

25. For example, in 1947, welfare workers rated below public school-teachers, but both occupations were above average in prestige (*Opinion News* 9 [September 1, 1947]). For a strongly favorable view of the contributions of the administrative state, see Emmette S. Redford, *Democracy in the Administrative State* (New York: Oxford University Press, 1969).

26. See Theodore Lowi, *The End of Liberalism,* 2d ed. (New York: W. W. Norton, 1979).

27. Warren E. Miller, Arthur H. Miller, and Edward J. Schneider, *American National Election Studies Data Sourcebook* (Cambridge: Harvard University Press, 1980), 171–90, 255–72.

28. See Friedman, *Capitalism and Freedom;* Arthur B. Laffer and Jan P. Seymour, *The Economics of the Tax Revolt* (New York: Harcourt Brace Jovanovich, 1979); and Michael Novak, *The American Vision: An Essay on the Future of Democratic Capitalism* (Washington, D.C.: American Enterprise Institute, 1978).

29. Goodsell, *Case for Bureaucracy,* 1–11.

30. Miller et al., *American National Election Studies Data Sourcebook.*

31. John J. Kirlin, "Policy Formulation," in *Making and Managing Policy: Formulation, Analysis, Evaluation,* ed. G. Ronald Gilbert (New York: Dekker, 1984), 21.

32. Ibid.

33. Woodrow Wilson, "The Study of Administration," in *The Administrative Process and Democratic Theory,* ed. Louis C. Gawthrop (Boston: Houghton Mifflin, 1970).

34. See Jameson W. Doig, " 'If I See a Murderous Fellow Sharpening a Knife Cleverly . . .': The Wilsonian Dichotomy and the Public Authority Tradition," *Public Administration Review* 43 (July/August 1983): 292–304.

35. Reinhard Bendix, *Max Weber: An Intellectual Portrait* (Garden City, N.Y.: Anchor Books, Doubleday and Company, 1962), 427.

36. Weber, *Economy and Society,* 2: 984.

37. Ibid., 980.

38. Herbert Kaufman, "Fear of Bureaucracy: A Raging Pandemic," *Public Administration Review* 41 (January/February 1981): 7.

39. Ibid.

40. Dwight Waldo, *The Enterprise of Public Administration* (Novato, Calif: Chandler and Sharp Publishers, 1980), 36.

41. Ibid., 37.

42. Ibid.

43. Ibid., 39–40.

44. Ibid., 43.

45. William G. Scott, "Barnard on the Nature of Elitist Responsibility," *Public Administration Review* 42 (May/June 1982): 197–201. See also David K. Hart and William G. Scott, "The Philosophy of American Management," *Southern Review of Public Administration* 6 (Summer 1982): 240–52.

46. Frederick C. Thayer, *An End to Hierarchy and Competition: Administration in the Post-Affluent World,* 2d ed. (New York: Franklin Watts, 1981).

47. Robert B. Denhardt, "Toward a Critical Theory of Public Organization," *Public Administration Review* 41 (November/December 1981): 628–35.

48. Scott, "Barnard on the Nature of Elitist Responsibility," 199.

49. Friedrich A. Hayek, *Individualism and Economic Order* (Chicago: University of Chicago Press, 1949), 1–32.

50. Ibid., 51.

51. Charles E. Lindblom, *Politics and Markets* (New York: Basic Books, 1977), 247–60, and Aaron Wildavsky, *Speaking Truth to Power: The Art and Craft of Policy Analysis* (Boston: Little, Brown and Company, 1979), 109–41.

52. See Michael M. Harmon, "Administrative Policy Formation and the Public Interest," *Public Administration Review* 24 (September/October 1969): 483–91; Frederick C. Mosher, "Professions in Public Service," *Public Administration Review* 38 (March/April 1978): 144–50; and Barry D. Karl, *Executive Reorganization and Reform in the New Deal* (Cambridge: Harvard University Press, 1963).

53. Hayek, *Individualism and Economic Order,* 14.

54. See Herbert J. Storing, "American Statesmanship: Old and New," in *Bureaucrats, Policy Analysts, Statesmen: Who Leads?* ed. Robert A. Goldwin (Washington, D.C.: American Enterprise Institute, 1980),

88–113; Diamond, "Ethics and Politics," 39–72; and William A. Schambra, "Martin Diamond's Doctrine of the American Regime," *Publius* 8 (Summer 1978): 213–18.

CHAPTER 2. CHARACTER, ADMINISTRATION, AND THE AMERICAN REGIME

1. Woodrow Wilson, "The Study of Administration," in *Public Administration, Politics, and the People: Selected Readings for Managers, Employees, and Citizens,* ed. Dean L. Yarwood (White Plains, N.Y.: Longman, 1987), 29.

2. The literature on these and related topics is extensive. For example, see Martin J. Schiesl, *The Politics of Efficiency: Municipal Administration and Reform in America* (Berkeley: University of California Press, 1977); Dwight Waldo, *The Administrative State* (New York: Ronald Press, 1948); Emmette S. Redford, *Democracy in the Administrative State* (New York: Oxford University Press, 1969); Barry Karl, *Executive Reorganization and Reform in the New Deal* (Cambridge: Harvard University Press, 1963); Paul H. Appleby, *Big Democracy* (New York: Alfred A. Knopf, 1949); Vincent Ostrom, *The Intellectual Crisis in American Public Administration* (University: University of Alabama Press, 1974); Paul Van Riper, *History of the United States Civil Service* (Chicago: Row, Peterson, 1958); Theodore Lowi, *The End of Liberalism,* 2d ed. (New York: W. W. Norton, 1979); and Laurence J. O'Toole, Jr., "American Public Administration and the Idea of Reform," *Administration and Society,* 16 (August 1984): 141–66.

3. Dwight Waldo, "The Perdurability of the Politics-Administration Dichotomy: Woodrow Wilson and the Identity Crisis in Public Administration," in *Politics and Administration: Woodrow Wilson and American Public Administration,* ed. Jack S. Rabin and James S. Bowman (New York: Dekker, 1984), 231, and Gerald E. Caiden, "In Search of an Apolitical Science of American Public Administration," in Rabin and Bowman, eds., *Politics and Administration,* 51–76.

4. Dwight Waldo, *The Enterprise of Public Administration* (Novato, Calif.: Chandler and Sharp Publishers, 1980), 10–12, 67–69.

5. Ibid., 66–67.

6. Ralph A. Rossum and Gary L. McDowell, eds., *The American Founding: Politics, Statesmanship, and the Constitution* (Port Washington, N.Y.: Kennikat Press, 1981).

7. Aristotle, *Politics,* ed. and trans. Ernest Baker (New York: Oxford University Press, 1934), 1279a24–b28.

8. To understand the extent to which we have discarded this view, think of the animosity our nation tends to have toward small-town life. Doesn't much of this aversion directly result from our recognition that in such towns the anonymity to which we have grown accustomed in large cities would be greatly reduced? In other words, in such places might "shame" and a "concern for one's reputation" play a much more forceful part in our everyday lives?

9. The distinctions between "confederations," "federations," and "unitary" forms of rule are important for this discussion. Basically, a confederation (such as we had under the Articles of Confederation or the South had under the Confederacy) preserves the sovereignty of its constituent members and has a weak central authority. In its most common form, the central authority cannot demand either wealth or people from its members; it must ask for them to be donated. (There are numerous examples from the Revolutionary War and the Civil War of the confederate authorities requesting troops from constituent states and being refused.)

A federation differs in one significant respect: it has direct power over individuals residing in the member states. (If the IRS wants a state's citizen for, say, nonpayment of federal taxes, it does not ask that the state authorities deliver up that person. The IRS sends its own agents to get the person in question.)

A unitary form of government generally has no intervening levels of lesser authorities (such as states, counties, or municipalities) between the central ruler and the citizen/subject. There is no shared sovereignty between it and any constituent members.

10. *Federalist Papers,* No. 72 (emphasis added).

11. An earlier variant of this view can be found in the first main section of the Declaration of Independence wherein Jefferson lists three of the "unalienable rights" possessed by all men. However, instead of following Locke's then well-known delineation of "life, liberty, and property," Jefferson chooses to substitute "pursuit of happiness" for "property." As its author clearly understood, history was replete with examples of regimes "captured" by one or the other religion that then attempted to impose its own vision of "happiness" on the inhabitants whose earthly fortunes were within its grasp. In all such cases, Jefferson and the other Founders thought that such imposed visions eventually resulted only in considerable misery for the subjects or citizens. Consequently, the inclusion of the phrase "pursuit of happiness" may be seen as a confession of ignorance by the Founders as to what would truly lead to earthly bliss. More important for our purposes, though, this famous phrase may be said to have laid the foundation for the much more explicit treatment presented in *Federalist* No. 10.

12. In this the Founders follow John Locke, the political philosopher who arguably had the most influence on their plan of government. See especially Sections 6 and 124 of "The Second Treatise of Civil Government: An Essay Concerning the True Original, Extent, and End of Civil Government," in his *Two Treatises of Government,* ed. Thomas I. Cook (New York: Hafner, 1947).

13. Leo Strauss contends that this sometimes frequent alliance between reason and the passions to control powerful desires is, in itself, a strong argument on behalf of the naturalness of tyranny (see Strauss, *On Tyranny* [Glencoe, Ill.: Free Press of Glencoe, 1963]).

14. For a discussion of this concept in a form available to the Founders, see Locke, "Second Treatise of Civil Government," chapter 5, and Adam Smith, *The Wealth of Nations,* ed. Edwin Cannan (New York: G. P. Putnam's Sons, 1904).

15. Once again, the Founders' reliance on the thought of Locke is evident here (see esp. chapter 5, "Of Property," in "Second Treatise").

16. By this Publius means, of course, the natural differences we may have in terms of raw intellect. But, more than this, he means the disproportionate shares we may have of such qualities as the willingness to work hard and to engage in high-risk activities. By self-selecting out of certain occupations (such as that of a fighter pilot or a salesman who works wholly on commission) for which we might be qualified but which we consider too risky or hard, we implicitly understand that we may be opting for a smaller annual income in another occupation. These wealth-oriented choices (many based on our own assumptions about our natures) commence quite early. Indeed, by the time we choose a major in college (pre-law over art, marketing over philosophy, pre-med over criminal justice, elementary education over engineering), we understand that our decisions are likely either to increase or decrease our probability of acquiring considerable wealth. In many cases, these choices are made because individuals value certain pursuits more highly than wealth. (Liberal education isn't always in vain!)

17. *Federalist Papers,* No. 10 (emphasis added). The manner in which our government has endeavored to protect such different faculties can readily be seen in the workings of our national patent and copyright offices. How much individual and national wealth has been amassed because an exceptionally gifted individual invented, for example, an artificial heart (or a personal computer) and then sought government protection of his "property right" in that item?

18. To appreciate the extent of our nation's progress in expanding the kinds of property within its embrace, consider the change that has occurred in just one occupation. At the time of the Founding, fully 96.6

percent of the inhabitants were in some way involved in farming. A more formidable majoritarian interest group could hardly have been devised. (The turmoil occasioned by Shays's Rebellion in Massachusetts, that uprising of farmers against their creditors, is not easily dismissed. So pervasive was the political power of the farmers that a militia could not be raised to march against them. Even George Washington—the head of the national government!—had great difficulty in putting together a force to suppress them.) Today those proportions are more than reversed. The 1990 census asserts that only some 2.6 percent of our fellow citizens are engaged in farming. The smallness of that figure is remarkable both for what it says about the modern reversal of the farmers' political power (think of the relatively dismal majoritarian support generated by such traumatic farming events as the Tractorcades of the 1970s or the family farm foreclosures of the 1980s) and for the immensity of the occupations that now subdivide us.

19. To understand this elementary point, one need only to think of the political firestorms that are ignited when counties or municipalities seeking additional property tax revenues reluctantly engage in widespread reevaluations of one common kind of property, namely, residential and commercial real estate. (In my own community of Atlanta, customarily docile citizens recently staged massive protest marches, organized lobbying groups, filed numerous class-action lawsuits, and so forth in their successful efforts to fight a clumsy, systemwide reevaluation.) Indeed, from one perspective it might be said that the government-encouraged growth in residential homeownership over the past sixty years—from about 33 percent in 1935 to some 66 percent today—created a powerful majority faction that is at odds with the intent of *Federalist* No. 10.

20. Although contemporary America is considerably larger and more populous than in the eighteenth century, it obviously has experienced enormous technological improvements in communication and transportation over the past 200-odd years. Nevertheless, the difficulty in forming effective national factions does not appear to have diminished significantly. For example, despite the marvelous improvements in the technology of communication—cellular phones, fax machines, personal computers, modems, television, and so on—even identifying the like-minded individuals of a potential faction proves almost insurmountably difficult. (How would one do it? Place advertisements in all the appropriate newspapers across the country? Place advertisements on CNN? Try to get exposure on national talk shows? Rent the mailing lists of appropriate journals and magazines? The efforts—and costs—involved are staggering.) Even if one could identify kindred members, where (and how) would they come together?

21. Abraham Lincoln, "Address Before the Young Men's Lyceum of Springfield, Illinois," in *The Collected Works of Abraham Lincoln,* ed. Roy P. Basler (New Brunswick, N.J.: Rutgers University Press, 1953), 1: 108–115.

22. For example, see Robert A. Goldwin, ed., *Bureaucrats, Policy Analysts, Statesmen: Who Leads?* (Washington, D.C.: American Enterprise Institute, 1980).

23. *Federalist Papers.*

24. Ibid., Nos. 1–4.

25. Herbert J. Storing, *What the Anti-Federalists Were For: The Political Thought of the Opponents of the Constitution* (Chicago: University of Chicago Press, 1981), 42–43.

26. As used throughout this book, the term "Founders" is intended to include both Federalists and Anti-Federalists. In short, it is used to encompass the works of those individuals who could be perceived as having had a significant influence on the issues discussed at the Constitutional Convention, regardless of whether they were on the winning (Federalist) side or not. For a treatment of the significance of this approach, see Storing, *What the Anti-Federalists Were For.*

27. Louis C. Gawthrop, "Civas, Civitas, and Civilitas: A New Focus for the Year 2000," *Public Administration Review* 44 (March 1984): 104.

28. For example, see the Special Edition, "Citizenship and Public Administration," *Public Administration Review* 44 (March 1984).

29. Gawthrop, "Civas," 101–7.

30. David K. Hart, "The Virtuous Citizen, the Honorable Bureaucrat, and 'Public' Administration," *Public Administration Review* 44 (March 1984): 111–20.

31. Ibid., 118.

32. H. George Frederickson and David K. Hart, "The Public Service and the Patriotism of Benevolence," *Public Administration Review* 45 (September/October 1985): 549, 551.

33. This view of the importance of nurturing the virtues of the citizenry is remarkably similar to some of the arguments advanced by the faction that did not prevail at the Constitutional Convention, namely, the Anti-Federalists. See Storing, *What the Anti-Federalists Were For,* esp. 20–23.

34. *Federalist Papers,* No. 51.

35. Martin Diamond, "The American Idea of Man: The View from the Founding," in *Critical Choices for Americans,* ed. Irving Kristol and Paul Weaver (Lexington, Mass.: Lexington Books, 1975), 2: 21.

36. *Federalist Papers,* 122–23. Publius continues in the same vein: "In framing a government, which is to be administered by men over men, the

great difficulty lies in this: You must first enable the government to control the governed; and in the next place, oblige it to control itself. A dependence on the people is, no doubt, the primary control on the government; but experience has taught mankind the necessity of auxiliary precautions."

37. Alexander Hamilton to Oliver Wolcott (June 29, 1798), in *Works,* ed. I. Lodge, 408, as cited in Lynton K. Caldwell, *The Administrative Theories of Hamilton and Jefferson* (Chicago: University of Chicago Press, 1944), 13.

38. For a brief but comprehensive introduction to this tradition, see the treatments of Machiavelli, Hobbes, and Locke in *History of Political Philosophy,* ed. Leo Strauss and Joseph Cropsey, 2d ed. (Chicago: Rand McNally College Publishing Company, 1971).

39. Martin Diamond, "Ethics and Politics: The American Way," in *The Moral Foundations of the American Republic,* ed. Robert Horwitz, 2d ed. (Charlottesville: University of Virginia Press, 1979), 47.

40. For example, see *Federalist Papers,* No. 6.

41. Herbert J. Storing, "American Statesmanship: Old and New," in Goldwin, ed., *Bureaucrats, Policy Analysts, Statesmen,* 92–93.

42. For example, see the treatment of this issue in Diamond, "Ethics and Politics," 39–72.

43. See John A. Rohr, *To Run a Constitution: The Legitimacy of the Administrative State* (Lawrence: University Press of Kansas, 1986), 1–10.

44. See Karl, *Executive Reorganization and Reform in the New Deal,* and Appleby, *Big Democracy.*

45. Diamond, "American Idea of Man," 2: 21–22.

CHAPTER 3. THE FOUNDERS, POLITICS, AND ADMINISTRATION

1. The term "Founders," intended to include both Federalists and Anti-Federalists, encompasses the works of those individuals who could be perceived as having had a significant influence on the issues discussed at the Constitutional Convention. For a treatment of the significance of this approach, see Herbert J. Storing, *What the Anti-Federalists Were For* (Chicago: University of Chicago Press, 1981).

2. Among the small number of scholars who have directed their attention to the Founders are John Rohr, *To Run a Constitution: The Legitimacy of the Administrative State* (Lawrence: University Press of Kansas, 1986), and Michael Spicer, *The Founders, the Constitution, and Public Administration: A Conflict in World Views* (Washington, D.C.: Georgetown University Press, 1995).

3. Given these intellectual and political origins of public administration, there is some irony in the fact that scholars in the field not only have contended that it was removed from the political context of the American republic but occasionally also presented it as an aristocratic haven for moral and intellectual excellence that *should* properly provide guidance for the rest of the citizens. For example, see H. George Frederickson and David K. Hart, "The Public Service and the Patriotism of Benevolence," *Public Administration Review* 45 (September/October 1985): 549ff.

4. Herbert J. Storing, "American Statesmanship: Old and New," in *Bureaucrats, Policy Analysts, Statesmen: Who Leads?* ed. Robert A. Goldwin (Washington, D.C.: American Enterprise Institute, 1980), 96–97 (emphasis added).

5. *Federalist Papers,* Nos. 1–4.

6. Storing, *What the Anti-Federalists Were For,* 42–43.

7. Lynton K. Caldwell, "Thomas Jefferson and Public Administration," *Public Administration Review* 3, 3 (1943): 241.

8. Ibid., 242.

9. Charles T. Goodsell, *The Case for Bureaucracy: A Public Administration Polemic* (Chatham, N.J.: Chatham House Publishers, 1983), 11.

10. In so doing, Jefferson may have erred in at least one respect. Rather than directing the attention of his passionately divided audience to the Constitution, that unifying document from which his presidential powers were derived, he directed the infant nation's gaze to these far less exalted "principles" of sound government. Jefferson thus became the first of a still-growing line of leaders who go outside the Constitution in quest of "better," "additional," or just "other" powers. (Think, for example, of the twentieth-century attention to electoral mandates.)

11. Caldwell, "Thomas Jefferson and Public Administration," 242–43.

12. L. K. Caldwell, "Alexander Hamilton: Advocate of Executive Leadership," *Public Administration Review* 4, 1 (1944): 113–26.

13. D. W. Martin, "The Fading Legacy of Woodrow Wilson," *Public Administration Review* 48 (March/April 1988): 632–33.

14. For example, see J. Rabin and James Bowman, eds., *Politics and Administration: Woodrow Wilson and American Public Administration* (New York: Dekker, 1984); Martin, "Fading Legacy of Wilson," 631–36; and Paul Van Riper, "The American Administrative State: Wilson and the Founders—An Unorthodox View," *Public Administration Review* 43 (November/December 1983): 477–90.

15. Martin, "Fading Legacy of Wilson," 634–35, and Dwight Waldo, *The Administrative State* (New York: Ronald Press, 1948): 97–100.

16. R. D. Miewald, "The Origins of Wilson's Thought—The German Tradition and the Organic State," in Rabin and Bowman, eds., *Politics and Administration,* 28.

17. Miewald, "Origins," 27–28.

18. Unfortunately for public administrators today, they are far too often treated as anything but models of enlightenment or virtue. The new Republican-ruled Congress, for example, seems to view the bureaucrats at best as misguided teenagers in clear need of a parental hand or at worst as hopelessly addled stepchildren who need to be restrained for the good of the community. As one step toward imposing more congressional control on administrators, Speaker Newt Gingrich has shepherded legislation through the House that would establish twice-monthly "corrections days." During these periods "questionable laws or regulations" could be corrected through expedited procedures. The Speaker sees this process as one that "will highlight the ability to cut back on particularly foolish or particularly destructive acts by the bureaucracy" (*Atlanta Constitution,* June 21, 1995, A8).

19. *Federalist Papers,* 435.

20. Jeremy Rabkin, "Bureaucratic Idealism and Executive Power: A Perspective on *The Federalist's* View of Public Administration," in *Saving the Revolution: The Federalist Papers and the American Founding,* ed. Charles Kesler (New York: Free Press, 1987), 196–98.

21. Gordon Wood, *The Creation of the American Republic, 1776–1787* (New York: Norton, 1969), 546.

22. Ibid., 598.

23. Rabkin, "Bureaucratic Idealism," 202.

24. This marvelous phrase has its origins in a comment Marvin Zetterbaum made in another context about Alexis de Tocqueville. However, its aptness to the present controversy is all too apparent, so I have appropriated it (see Zetterbaum, *Tocqueville and the Problem of Democracy* [Stanford, Calif.: Stanford University Press, 1967]).

25. No political problem appears more often in more guises than that of "justice." Though frequently ignored or violated, its basic tenets (and their foundation in inequality) have been a subject of open scrutiny for millennia. If one wishes to recognize the presence of "natural" inequalities within the regime and link them to the common good, one makes the revered values of the community—wealth, honor, position, and so forth—proportionate to an individual's contributions to that community. In short, "equal things to equals." Conversely, if one wishes to dampen and diminish the influence of such "natural" inequalities in the regime, one provides a system of compensatory distribution that diminishes the ability of the superior to acquire disproportionate shares of the valued entities and, instead, channels more of them to the less favored. ("Equal things to unequals.") For an overview of these approaches, see Aristotle, *The Nicomachean Ethics,* trans. H. Rackham (Cambridge: Harvard University Press, 1934); Plato, *The Republic,* trans. Allan Bloom (New York: Basic

Books, 1968); and Aristophanes, *Lysistrata,* ed. Jeffrey Henderson (New York: Oxford University Press, 1987).

26. In my own experience, public employees at all levels of government—and in Atlanta, my university has a large and gratifying mix of graduate students who are in-service employees from the national, state, and local governments—frequently balk at this broad characterization of discretion. With some regularity, my students will take refuge in the notion that they are not "public administrators" and, therefore, that they have absolutely minimal discretion to exercise. Yet, as they come to concede, even public employees meeting the citizenry at the local Social Security or Division of Motor Vehicles (DMV) office are in a position to facilitate or hinder a request for service simply by the expedient of how they treat the application. One almost never has the discretion to deny a benefit to a citizen merely because that person is rude, obnoxious, and angry; however, the applications of such individuals conceivably might be processed a bit more slowly.

27. For example, one of the early targets of the previously mentioned "corrections day" in the House was an Occupational Safety and Health Administration (OSHA) regulation requiring the presence of at least four firefighters—"two inside and two out—before any firefighters can enter a burning building" (*Atlanta Constitution,* June 21, 1995, A8). One can easily see the good intent of the OSHA regulators (elevating the protection of firefighters over that of the threatened property), but one can also see the impracticality of such a hard-and-fast rule for firefighting. Sometimes administrators may need a reminder about the need to presume that the professionals at the scene of an unpredictable event are reliably rational and in possession of good judgment—judgment to which the administrators simply must defer.

28. The change in the ways by which we select public administrators over the past 130 or so years is almost traceable by the variation in the titles that such administrators prefer. Thus, the aptly named public servant of the patronage era gives way to the civil servant of the reform movement who, in turn, became the government or public employee of contemporary times. The changes in titles were conscious efforts to reflect what administrators considered to be appropriate relationships between themselves and the citizenry.

Though not discussed here, the counterpart change in the way administrators are supposed to view the citizenry is, in some ways, much more troubling. The move from the blatantly political title of citizen to the slightly less one of constituent has undergone a well-known third change: to that of the market-oriented client or consumer. This last change is intended to emulate commercial business and, ironically, to foster a service mentality more than a little reminiscent of the patronage era (but totally devoid of the obvious political context that administrators of that time openly embraced). The most popular proponent of this approach, of course, is the fiscal bible of Vice-President Al Gore: David Osborne and Ted Gabler's *Reinventing Government: How the Entrepreneurial Spirit Is Transforming the Public Sector from Schoolhouse to Statehouse, City Hall to the Pentagon* (New York: Addison-Wesley Publishing Company, 1992).

29. See Storing, "American Statesmanship," 88–113.

30. Undoubtedly our best and most famous expression of this sentiment is found in the Declaration of Independence (the source of these words).

31. Insofar as America is concerned, the most influential theoretical treatment of majority rule is found in the second of John Locke's *Two Treatises of Government*, ed. Thomas I. Cook (New York: Hafner Press, 1947).

32. Perhaps we might be excused a little for concentrating so much on only one source of legitimacy. Not only is it the political basis of our own regime, but its worldwide influence has grown to such an extent that almost no established nation or international entity will extend diplomatic recognition (and the attendant economic and political benefits that accompany it) to a government that has not demonstrated it has the support of its citizens/subjects by holding elections. (The elections do not have to be "fair"; they just have to produce a winner. Thus, the world witnessed Castro holding his first parliamentary elections in thirty-five years with only one candidate for each available seat. Similarly, significant levels of fraud may mar the elections in Iran, Mexico, Nicaragua, the Philippines, and Haiti, but they are nonetheless still considered an acceptable source of the political powers subsequently wielded by the winners. Indeed, in almost every case these flawed events are the only real alternative to the obvious recourse to force.)

33. A citzenry's truthful answer to the ancient Spartan question, "Who are your heroes?" provides an important initial insight into the dominant character of the regime. The response, of course, will properly vary according to the type of regime in which one lives. In a democratic republic such as our own, the answers—detailed in everything from the public statuary adorning a city to the famous pictures of MLK or JFK reverentially gracing the parlor wall of a private home—generally involve individuals who in various ways embody important regime values. These values could be the equality a given hero so fought to promote, the liberties he or she attempted to establish, or even the salutary virtue of compassion that personified the individual's life. (A hero certainly does not have to be a member of the regime. Mother Teresa amply represents the virtue of compassion to large numbers of Americans.) Though there are exceptions to the rule, our sports heroes tend to embody low-level virtues

the citizens think worth emulating. (Clearly, bad boy mavericks such as tennis great John McEnroe may reach prominence because of their unsurpassed skills, but one does not envision mentors of the sport advising their young wards to emulate the obnoxious behavior of such victors.)

The serious concerns about a decline in character arise when substantial numbers of the citizenry come to profess admiration for individuals who seem to embody traits that are more often associated with another type of regime. Thus, if instead of Babe Ruth in sports, Cary Grant in films, or Abraham Lincoln in politics our citizens openly praised antidemocrats such as Fidel Castro or Julius Caesar, there would be major cause for concern about the present and future health of the nation. (In the case of America, political leaders such as Bob Dole and thoughtful gadflies such as William Bennett have joined those individuals raising major public concerns about the vicious, hate-filled lyrics of various recording artists. The criticisms extended to attacks on Time-Warner Corporation, which seems to be one of the most visible producers of so many of the offending materials.)

34. Obvious examples would be Sen. Bill Bradley, a former basketball star, and Jack Kemp, a professional football quarterback who parlayed his fame into a seat in Congress and the secretaryship of Housing and Urban Development (HUD).

35. For example, the contemporary ability of the Kennedy family's name to influence elections (especially in Massachusetts) is widely acknowledged. Similarly, there have been clear electoral advantages attached to being a Rockefeller.

36. See Alexis de Tocqueville's treatment of this issue in *Democracy in America*, ed. J. P. Mayer (Garden City, N.Y.: Anchor Books, 1969).

37. With the daily images of military force being used to establish issues of "Who says?" in Bosnia, Somalia, Chechnya, and elsewhere, Americans have visible reminders of its periodic significance for the settlement of important political questions. Similarly, we have seen the Ayatollah Khomeini originally assert that he deserved to rule in post-Shah Iran by virtue of divine right. For a devoted population, such assertions are powerful and extraordinarily difficult to challenge. (Indeed, messianic leaders of religious sects in America—the controversial David Koresh of the Branch Davidians comes readily to mind—sometimes cement their claim to rule by means of asserting a special relationship with God.) At least in terms of mass appeal, though, a claim to rule because of superior wisdom is much more tenuous. In what is undoubtedly the most famous theoretical discussion of this claim, Plato's *Republic,* Socrates concedes the near-impossibility of there ever being a convergence of wisdom and political rule by presenting his discussion in the guise of a "city in speech."

38. See Arthur S. Fleming, "The Civil Servant in a Period of Transition," *Public Administration Review* 13, 2 (1953): 77. For slightly more equivocal treatments of the issue, see Paul H. Appleby, "Toward Better Public Administration," *Public Administration Review* 7, 2 (1947): 93–99, and David M. Levitan, "The Neutrality of the Public Service," *Public Administration Review* 2, 4 (1942): 317–23 (esp. 320).

39. One of the better examinations of this Germanic influence is found in Albert Somit and Joseph Tannenhause, *The Development of American Political Science: From Burgess to Behavioralism* (New York: Irvington Publishers, 1982), which explores the origins of contemporary American political science.

40. For a discussion of this evolutionary quest to become wise in public administration, see Herbert J. Storing, "Leonard D. White and the Study of Public Administration," *Public Administration Review* 25 (March 1965): 38–51; Herman Finer, "Democratic Responsibility in Democratic Government," *Public Administration Review* 1, 4 (1941): 335–50; and Storing, "American Statesmanship," 88–113.

41. The attraction of this combination of expertise and political neutrality is no small matter and can be seen in the way the pendulum continues to swing back and forth as communities vacillate between professional managers and mayors (or commissioners) in numerous county and city governments.

CHAPTER 4. PUBLIC VIRTUE, HONOR,
AND REPUTATION

1. John Adams to Samuel Adams (1790), in *Political Thought in America: An Anthology,* ed. Michael B. Levy (Homewood, Ill.: Dorsey Press, 1982), 73.

2. *To Serve with Honor: Report of the President's Commission on Federal Ethics Law Reform* (Petersburg, Va.: Unicor Print Plant, 1989), 1. The critical distinction between being honorable and acting honorably is discussed in this chapter.

3. Forrest McDonald, *Novus Ordo Seclorum: The Intellectual Origins of the Constitution* (Lawrence: University Press of Kansas, 1985), 70–71.

4. Martin Diamond, "Ethics and Politics: The American Way," in *The Moral Foundations of the American Republic,* ed. Robert Horwitz, 2d ed. (Charlottesville: University of Virginia Press, 1979), 47.

5. Max Farrand, ed., *The Records of the Federal Convention of 1787* (New Haven: Yale University Press, 1937), 1: 82 (emphasis added); see also McDonald, *Novus Ordo Seclorum,* 188–89.

6. Martin Diamond, "The Federalist," in *American Political Thought: The Philosophic Dimension of American Statesmanship,* ed. Morton J. Frisch and Richard G. Stevens, 2d ed. (Itasca, Ill.: F. E. Peacock, 1983), 87.

7. Robert H. Horwitz, "John Locke and the Preservation of Liberty: A Perennial Problem of Civic Education," in his *Moral Foundations of the American Republic,* 132–33 (emphasis added).

8. Diamond, "Federalist," 88.

9. Diamond, "Ethics and Politics," 56ff.

10. McDonald, *Novus Ordo Seclorum,* 188–91.

11. *Federalist Papers,* No. 57, 350.

12. John Adams to Samuel Adams (1790), in Levy, ed., *Political Thought in America,* 73.

13. Herbert J. Storing, *What the Anti-Federalists Were For: The Political Thought of the Opponents of the Constitution* (Chicago: University of Chicago Press, 1981), 8.

14. Ibid., 15–23.

15. Ibid., 21.

16. Ibid. To understand arguments over virtue in the new regime, it helps to clarify the distinction between virtue per se and "political" (or "public") virtue. The former is understood to mean the actual possession of a particular attribute that is laudable, such as moderation. The crucial aspect of such a possession is that one acts moderately because one esteems moderation for itself. Political virtue is different in that, although one may act moderately, one does so primarily because of the public honor or reputation attached to such a display.

17. Ibid., 20.

18. Samuel Bryan, "Letter of Centinel, No. 1" (1787), in Levy, ed., *Political Thought in America,* 115 (emphasis added). Indeed, it was this perceived need for a more or less egalitarian division of property that demonstrated how thoroughly the more idyllic regime contemplated by the Anti-Federalists was at odds with the plans of their Federalist opponents. A regime founded on the unleashing of acquisitiveness almost by definition is going to have substantial inequality of property. (After all, this was the essence of John Locke's argument in the second of his *Two Treatises of Government,* the work that so heavily influenced the founding of the American regime.) Equality among the citizenry may indeed be fostered by minimizing the differences in the accumulation of private property, but a successful formula for such minimalization has certainly proven elusive throughout history. For some of the more interesting treatments of this subject, see Aristotle's *Politics,* ed. and trans. Ernest Barker (New York: Oxford University Press, 1946); Plutarch's "Lycurgus," in *The Quest for Justice,* ed. L. G. Rubin and C. T. Rubin (Needham Heights,

Mass.: Ginn Press, 1987), 11–33; and Bertrand de Jouvenel's *The Ethics of Redistribution* (Cambridge: Cambridge University Press, 1952).

19. *Federalist Papers,* No. 10, esp. 78–79. See also Diamond, "Ethics and Politics," 39–72.

20. *Federalist Papers,* No. 51, 322.

21. Robert A. Goldwin, "Of Men and Angels: A Search for Morality in the Constitution," in *Moral Foundations of the American Republic,* 10.

22. John Rohr, *Ethics for Bureaucrats: An Essay on Law and Values* (New York: Dekker, 1978), esp. 59 and 64–74.

23. Stephen K. Bailey, "Ethics and the Public Service," in *Public Administration and Democracy,* ed. Roscoe C. Martin (Syracuse, N.Y.: Syracuse University Press, 1965), 283–98.

24. McDonald, *Novus Ordo Seclorum,* 189.

25. Ibid., 223.

26. Ibid., 198 (emphasis added). An elaboration of this treatment of "honor"—one that, developing the case of Washington, takes issue with McDonald's stress on public opinion as an appropriate guide for honorable republicans—is found in Lorraine Smith Pangle and Thomas L. Pangle, "Washington and the Principle of Honor," in their *Learning of Liberty: The Educational Ideas of the American Founders* (Lawrence: University Press of Kansas, 1993), 231–49.

27. McDonald, *Novus Ordo Seclorum,* 198–99.

28. Aristotle, *Nicomachean Ethics,* trans. H. Rackham (Cambridge: Harvard University Press, 1934), 1123a33–1125a35.

29. In the context of lauding the necessity of standing for frequent elections in America, Alexis de Tocqueville argues that politicians thereby could acquire certain democratic virtues (see his *Democracy in America,* ed. J. P. Mayer [Garden City, N.Y.: Anchor Books, 1969], 509–13).

30. Pangle and Pangle, "Washington," 242–49.

31. Adam Smith, *The Theory of Moral Sentiments* (Indianapolis: Liberty Classics, 1976), 208.

32. Ibid., 208–9.

33. Robert H. Horwitz, "John Locke," 139ff. For a fascinating discussion of the rise in "shamelessness" within our culture, see Christopher Lasch, *The Revolt of the Elites and the Betrayal of Democracy* (New York: W. W. Norton, 1995).

34. Charles T. Goodsell, *The Case for Bureaucracy: A Public Administration Polemic* (Chatham, N.J.: Chatham House Publishers, 1983).

35. John A. Rohr, *To Run a Constitution: The Legitimacy of the Administrative State* (Lawrence: University Press of Kansas, 1986).

36. Bruce Adams, "The Frustrations of Government Service," *Public Administration Review* 44 (January/February 1984): 5.

37. Woodrow Wilson, "The Study of Administration," in *Public Administration, Politics, and the People: Selected Readings for Managers, Employees, and Citizens,* ed. Dean Yarwood (White Plains, N.Y.: Longman, 1987), 26.

38. Ibid., 27.

39. Ibid. (emphasis added).

40. Dwight Waldo, *The Enterprise of Public Administration* (Novato, Calif.: Chandler and Sharp Publishers, 1980), 61–62, 77–78.

41. *American Society for Public Administration Code of Ethics and Implementation Guidelines,* Supplement to *P.A. Times* (May 1, 1985); John A. Rohr, "The Study of Ethics in the P.A. Curriculum," *Public Administration Review* 36 (July/August 1976): 398–406; Joel L. Fleishman, Lance Liebman, and Mark H. Moore, eds., *Public Duties: The Moral Obligations of Government Officials* (Cambridge: Harvard University Press, 1981); Rohr, *Ethics for Bureaucrats,* 50–51; and Ralph Clark Chandler, "The Problem of Moral Reasoning in American Public Administration: The Case for a Code of Ethics," *Public Administration Review* 43 (January/February 1983): 32–39.

42. Stephen K. Bailey, "Ethics and the Public Service," in *Public Administration: Concepts and Cases,* ed. Richard J. Stillman II, 3d ed. (Boston: Houghton Mifflin, 1984), 480–89.

43. Frederick C. Mosher, "The Professional State," in Yarwood, ed., *Public Administration, Politics, and the People,* 198.

44. Not coincidentally, one of the contemporary solutions to the citizenry's perception that their governors too often are acting in a self-interested manner has been to push for what one might call an Aristotelian remedy: term limits. By demanding that there be a limit on the service of "professional politicians," the citizenry is advocating in effect a variant of Aristotle's principle of "rule and be ruled" in turn. The degree to which citizen dissatisfaction has spread to the roles of public administrators is seen in the sentiments occasionally being expressed that such limitations should also be extended to the ranks of the public service. (In essence, this reaction amounts to a rather ill-considered repudiation of the accomplishments public administration has made in the past century, for it is tantamount to a call for a return to the democratic patronage system discussed in chapter 3.)

45. See Louis C. Gawthrop, "Civas, Civitas, and Civilitas: A New Focus for the Year 2000," *Public Administration Review* 44 (March/April 1984): 101–7; David K. Hart, "The Virtuous Citizen, the Honorable Bureaucrat, and 'Public' Administration," in *Public Administration Review* 44 (March 1984): 111–20; David K. Hart, "The Honorable Bureaucrat Among the Philistines," *Administration and Society* 15 (May 1983): 43–48; H. G. Frederickson and David K. Hart, "The Public Service and

the Patriotism of Benevolence," *Public Administration Review* 45 (September/October 1985): 547–53; and Rohr, *Ethics for Bureaucrats.*
   46. On these and related topics, see Dwight Waldo, *The Administrative State,* 2d ed. (New York: Holmes and Meier, 1984), ix–lxiv; Waldo, *Enterprise of Public Administration,* 49–64; H. George Frederickson, *New Public Administration* (University: University of Alabama Press, 1980), 93–111; and Phillip J. Cooper, "The Wilsonian Dichotomy in Administrative Law," in *Politics and Administration: Woodrow Wilson and American Public Administration,* ed. J. Rabin and J. Bowman (New York: Dekker, 1984), 79–94.
   47. Joel L. Fleishman, "Self-Interest and Political Integrity," in Fleishman, Liebman, and Moore, eds., *Public Duties,* 70–71.

CHAPTER 5. EDUCATING THE GOVERNORS

   1. Plutarch, "Lycurgus," in *The Quest for Justice: Readings in Political Ethics,* ed. Leslie G. Rubin and Charles T. Rubin (Needham Heights, Mass.: Ginn Press, 1987), 11–33.
   2. In addition to the political expressions such dissatisfaction has found in the candidacy of Ross Perot and in the rhetoric before (and after) the 1994 congressional elections, see Christopher Lasch, *The Revolt of the Elites and the Betrayal of Democracy* (New York: W. W. Norton, 1995); Jean Bethke Elshtain, *Democracy on Trial* (New York: Basic Books, 1995); and Michael Kazin, *The Populist Persuasion: An American History* (New York: Basic Books, 1995).
   3. *Federalist Papers,* 72.
   4. NASPAA Commission on Peer Review and Accreditation, *Self-Study Report Instructions* (Washington, D.C., July 1994), 12.
   5. MPA Degree Program, School of Public Administration and Urban Studies, *Georgia State University Graduate Bulletin, College of Public and Urban Affairs, 1995–96,* 68.
   6. For these reasons, it is not hard to see why the Spartan model was an attractive theoretical standard for advocates of classical republicanism.
   7. Although there are inherent problems with cross-cultural comparisons, the history of Japan provides an extreme example of the operation of shame; there the loss of face (being exposed to the disapproval of one's fellow citizens after committing some dishonorable act) can cause individuals to resign their positions in disgrace and, occasionally, still take their own lives.
   8. Herbert J. Storing quoting Maryland Farmer VI, 5.I.82, in *What the Anti-Federalists Were For: The Political Thought of the Opponents of the Constitution* (Chicago: University of Chicago Press, 1981), 21.

9. For an elaboration of this argument on the implications of Locke's theory for sexual equality, see Diana Schaub's review of *The Learning of Liberty,* in *Academic Questions* 8, 2 (Spring 1995): 93–98.

10. Robert H. Horwitz, "John Locke and the Preservation of Liberty: A Perennial Problem of Civic Education," in his *Moral Foundations of the American Republic,* 2d ed. (Charlottesville: University Press of Virginia, 1979), 129–56. See also James L. Axtell, ed., *The Educational Writings of John Locke* (Cambridge: Cambridge University Press, 1968), and John Locke, *Some Thoughts Concerning Education,* ed. F. W. Garforth (Woodbury, N.Y.: Barron's Educational Series, 1964).

11. Horwitz, "Locke and the Preservation of Liberty," 141.

12. Ibid.

13. Locke's approach to the connections between self-interest and public virtue also found expression in Alexis de Tocqueville's concept of self-interest properly understood: "That by serving his fellows man serves himself in that doing good is to his private advantage. . . . If it does not lead the will directly to virtue, it establishes habits which unconsciously turn it that way" (*Democracy in America,* ed. J. P. Mayer [Garden City, N.Y.: Anchor Books, 1969], 525 and 527).

14. Horwitz, "Locke and the Preservation of Liberty," 154–55.

15. An excellent discussion of some of these points is found in Lorraine Smith Pangle and Thomas L. Pangle, *The Learning of Liberty: The Educational Ideas of the American Founders* (Lawrence: University Press of Kansas, 1993), 91–105.

16. Ibid., 92.

17. A summarization of Samuel Knox's thought is provided in ibid.

18. A thorough discussion of the American difficulty with conscription, armies, and war is provided by Tocqueville in *Democracy in America,* 22–23 and 645–64.

19. David Tucker, "The Political Thought of Thomas Jefferson's *Notes on the State of Virginia,*" in *The American Founding: Politics, Statesmanship, and the Constitution,* ed. Ralph A. Rossum and Gary L. McDowell (Port Washington, N.Y.: Kennikat Press, 1981), 116.

20. Lynton K. Caldwell, *The Administrative Theories of Hamilton and Jefferson: Their Contribution to Thought on Public Administration* (Chicago: University of Chicago Press, 1944), 110.

21. Thomas Jefferson to James Madison, in *The Papers of Thomas Jefferson,* ed. Julian P. Boyd et al. (Princeton: Princeton University Press, 1950), 12: 442 (emphasis added).

22. "Bill 79 of 1779 for the 'More General Diffusion of Knowledge,' " in *Thomas Jefferson and the Development of American Public Education,* ed. James B. Conant (Berkeley: University of California Press, 1962), 88–93.

23. Thomas Jefferson, *Notes on the State of Virginia,* ed. William Peden (New York: W. W. Norton, 1972), 146–49. For an argument that the *Notes* represent an Aristotelian-like detailing of the proper requisites for the new regime, see William D. Richardson, "Thomas Jefferson and Race: The Declaration and *Notes on the State of Virginia," Polity* 16 (Spring 1984): 447–66.

24. Thomas Jefferson to John Adams, October 28, 1813, *The Adams-Jefferson Letters,* ed. Lester J. Cappon, 2 vols. (Chapel Hill: University of North Carolina Press, 1959).

25. Quoted in Pangle and Pangle, *Learning of Liberty,* 110.

26. "Report of the Commissioners to Fix the Site of the University of Virginia, August 1, 1818," in Conant, ed., *Jefferson and Public Education,* 127–38. This whole program also has some successors in the works of thoughtful individuals such as Sir Henry Taylor, who advocated a comprehensive education for public servants in the nineteenth century. See Taylor's *The Statesman,* ed. David Lewis Schaefer and Roberta Rubel Schaefer (Westport, Conn.: Praeger, 1992).

27. Pangle and Pangle, *Learning of Liberty,* 78.

28. Tocqueville makes a similar laudatory comment about the educational legacy of this region in *Democracy in America,* 35 and 45–47.

29. Pangle and Pangle, *Learning of Liberty,* 76.

30. Ibid., 89.

31. Woodrow Wilson, "The Study of Administration," in *Public Administration, Politics, and the People: Selected Readings for Managers, Employees, and Citizens,* ed. Dean L. Yarwood (White Plains, N.Y.: Longman, 1987), 27.

32. Dwight Waldo, "The Perdurability of the Politics-Administration Dichotomy: Woodrow Wilson and the Identity Crisis in Public Administration," in *Politics and Administration: Woodrow Wilson and American Public Administration,* ed. Jack S. Rabin and James S. Bowman (New York: Dekker, 1984), 225.

33. Ibid., 230–31.

34. Wilson, "Study of Administration," 27.

CHAPTER 6. THE AMERICAN CHARACTER
AND PUBLIC POLICY

1. See Martin Diamond, "The American Idea of Man: The View from the Founding," in *Critical Choices for Americans,* ed. Irving Kristol and Paul Weaver (Lexington, Mass.: Lexington Books, 1975), vol. 2; Irving Kristol, " 'When Virtue Loses All Her Loveliness'—Some Reflections on Capitalism and 'The Free Society,' " *Public Interest* 21 (Fall 1970): 3–15;

and Milton Friedman and Rose Friedman, *Free to Choose: A Personal Statement* (New York: Harcourt Brace Jovanovich, 1980). The character traits I will be discussing are not mutually exclusive and overlap considerably, especially in the writings of the Founders. For a discussion of the rise of the American administrative state, see Paul P. Van Riper, "The American Administrative State: Wilson and the Founders—An Unorthodox View," *Public Administration Review* 43 (November/December 1983): 477–90, and Dwight Waldo, *The Enterprise of Public Administration* (Novato, Calif.: Chandler and Sharp Publishers, 1980).

2. See Milton Friedman, *Capitalism and Freedom* (Chicago: University of Chicago Press, 1962); George Gilder, *Wealth and Poverty* (New York: Basic Books, 1981); Thomas Sowell, *Markets and Minorities* (New York: Basic Books, 1981); Bernard J. Frieden, "The New Regulation Comes to Suburbia," *Public Interest* 55 (Spring 1979): 15–27; and, of course, Adam Smith, *The Wealth of Nations,* ed. Edwin Cannan (New York: G. P. Putnam's Sons, 1904). See also Robert A. Goldwin and William A. Schambra, eds., *How Democratic Is the Constitution?* (Washington: American Enterprise Institute, 1980); and Goldwin and Schambra, eds., *How Capitalistic Is the Constitution?* (Washington: American Enterprise Institute, 1982).

3. The term "liberal" is here used not in its contemporary political connotation but in the proper tradition of political philosophy, wherein the ideas of John Locke and his successors that were adopted by the Founders are seen as modern, novel, and enlightened. The doctrines of "natural rights," "just powers" derived only from the "consent of the governed," limited government, and the protection of private property were intended to enhance the liberties and security of the individual.

4. In addition to individualism, acquisitiveness, and concern for reputation, the Founders also considered the importance of such traits as civility, moderation, and courage. For a general discussion of these qualities, see Gabriel A. Almond and Sidney Verba, *The Civic Culture* (Princeton: Princeton University Press, 1963), and Wilson Carey McWilliams, "On Equality as the Moral Foundation for Community," in *The Moral Foundations of the American Republic,* ed. Robert Horwitz, 2d ed. (Charlottesville: University of Virginia Press, 1979), 183–213. The concept of moderation falls within the general idea of "justice," especially that part of it known as distributive justice. For an introduction to the topic, see Aristotle, *Nicomachean Ethics* (1934; rpt. Cambridge: Harvard University Press, 1975), book 5, chap. 3, and Plato, *The Republic,* trans. Allan Bloom (New York: Basic Books, 1968), esp. book 4. On courage or "risk taking," see the works of Adam Smith, esp. his *Theory of Moral Sentiments,* ed. D. D. Raphael and A. L. Macfie (Indianapolis: Liberty Classics, 1976).

5. See Alexis de Tocqueville, *Democracy in America,* ed. J. P. Mayer (Garden City, N.Y.: Anchor Books, 1969), 506–13; Robert A. Goldwin, "Of Men and Angels: A Search for Morality in the Constitution," in Horwitz, ed., *The Moral Foundations of the American Republic,* 1–18; Martin Diamond, "Ethics and Politics: The American Way," in Horwitz, ed., *Moral Foundations,* 39–72; and Robert H. Horwitz, "John Locke and the Preservation of Liberty: A Perennial Problem of Civic Education," in Horwitz, ed., *Moral Foundations,* 129–56.

6. See John E. Parsons, Jr., "Locke's Doctrine of Property," *Social Research* 36, 3 (1969): 389–411; Henry Moulds, "Private Property in John Locke's State of Nature," *American Journal of Economics and Sociology* 23 (1964): 179–88; Smith, *Wealth of Nations;* Joseph Cropsey, "'Capitalist' Liberalism" and "The Invisible Hand: Moral and Political Considerations," in Joseph Cropsey, *Political Philosophy and the Issues of Politics* (Chicago: University of Chicago Press, 1980), 53–75 and 76–89; Diamond, "Ethics and Politics," 39–72; and *Federalist Papers,* No. 10 (Madison).

7. This idea that matters of reputation control behavior and lead individuals to act in the public interest has been addressed by thinkers as diverse as Plato and Locke. In the liberal tradition, see James L. Axtell, ed., *The Educational Writings of John Locke* (Cambridge: Cambridge University Press, 1968).

8. See, for example, Richard Hofstadter, "The Founding Fathers: An Age of Realism," in Horwitz, ed., *Moral Foundations,* 73–85.

9. *Federalist Papers,* 322.

10. See, for example, Leo Strauss, "Plato," and Robert A. Goldwin, "John Locke," in *History of Political Philosophy,* ed. Leo Strauss and Joseph Cropsey, 2d ed. (Chicago: Rand McNally College Publishing Company, 1972), 7–63, 451–86.

11. Diamond, "Ethics and Politics," 47.

12. Ibid., 48.

13. Friedman, *Capitalism and Freedom,* 27.

14. Tocqueville, *Democracy in America,* 246–61, 506–17, and 604–5.

15. Ibid., 515 (emphasis added).

16. Ibid., 510, 520–24.

17. Ibid., 515, 673.

18. See Smith, *Wealth of Nations;* the second of John Locke's *Two Treatises of Government* (New York: Hafner, 1947); and the derivative thoughts of Friedman, *Capitalism and Freedom.*

19. James Boswell, *Boswell's Life of Johnson* (London: Oxford University Press, 1934), 2: 323.

20. F. A. Hayek, *Individualism and Economic Order* (Chicago: University of Chicago Press, 1949), 12.

21. Friedman, *Capitalism and Freedom,* 27. The influence of Friedman on the policies of the contemporary Republican Congress is striking. See Ed Gillespie and Bob Schellhas, eds., *Contract with America* (New York: Times Books, 1995).

22. Friedman, *Capitalism and Freedom,* 9.

23. For example, see Wilson Carey McWilliams, "Democracy and the Citizen: Community, Dignity, and the Crisis of Contemporary Politics in America," in Goldwin and Schambra, eds., *How Democratic Is the Constitution?* 79–101, and Forrest McDonald, "The Constitution and Hamiltonian Capitalism," in Goldwin and Schambra, eds., *How Capitalistic Is the Constitution?* 49–74. See also Friedman, *Capitalism and Freedom;* Gilder, *Wealth and Poverty;* Sowell, *Markets and Minorities;* Bernard J. Frieden, "The New Regulation Comes to Suburbia," 15–27; and, of course, Smith, *Wealth of Nations.*

24. *Federalist Papers,* 16–24, and Diamond, "Ethics and Politics," 39–72.

25. Gilder, *Wealth and Poverty,* 105–13.

26. Ibid., 112.

27. Perhaps the most renowned treatment of this arrangement is to be found in Plato's *Republic,* wherein the Philosopher King, with the help of his carefully selected and educated Guardians, oversees every significant aspect of the regime.

28. Emmette S. Redford, *Democracy in the Administrative State* (New York: Oxford University Press, 1969), 52–60.

29. Charles Lindblom, *Politics and Markets* (New York: Basic Books, 1977), 247–60, and Aaron Wildavsky, *Speaking Truth to Power: The Art and Craft of Policy Analysis* (Boston: Little, Brown and Company, 1979).

30. The collective or public good on whose behalf the vertical or hierarchical controls are frequently sought can be noble (if seldom attainable), such as in the quest for excellence by both the individual and the regime. See Aristotle's *Nicomachean Ethics.*

31. Lindblom, *Politics and Markets,* 276–90.

32. *Federalist Papers,* 16–24; and W. Burnham, "The Constitution, Capitalism, and the Need for Rationalized Regulation," in Goldwin and Schambra, eds., *How Capitalistic Is the Constitution?* 75–105.

33. Tocqueville, *Democracy in America,* 506.

34. Ibid.

35. Ibid., 506–7, 510–13, and 525–28.

36. A. Young, "Conservatives, the Constitution, and the 'Spirit of Accommodation,' " in Goldwin and Schambra, eds., *How Capitalistic Is the Constitution?* 117–47.

37. *Federalist Papers,* 16–24.

38. Ibid., 10–15, 45–56, and 127–41.

39. Herbert Storing, "American Statesmanship: Old and New," in *Bureaucrats, Policy Analysts, Statesmen: Who Leads?* ed. Robert Goldwin (Washington, D.C.: American Enterprise Institute, 1980), 92–93.

40. Diamond, "Ethics and Politics," 71.

41. See Barry Dean Karl, *Executive Reorganization and Reform in the New Deal* (Cambridge: Harvard University Press, 1963); James M. Landis, *The Administrative Process* (Westport, Conn.: Greenwood Press, 1974); Kenneth Culp Davis, *Discretionary Justice: A Preliminary Inquiry* (Baton Rouge: Louisiana State University Press, 1969); Emmette S. Redford, *Administration of National Economic Control* (New York: Macmillan, 1972); and Phillip J. Cooper, *Public Law and Public Administration* (Palo Alto, Calif.: Mayfield Publishing Company, 1983), 215–32.

42. Dwight Waldo, *The Administrative State* (New York: Ronald Press, 1948), 104–29.

43. James Q. Wilson, ed., *The Politics of Regulation* (New York: Basic Books, 1980); Paul H. Appleby, *Big Democracy* (New York: Alfred A. Knopf, 1949); George Frederickson, "The Recovery of Civism in Public Administration," *Public Administration Review* 42, 6 (November/December 1982): 501–8; David Mathews, "The Public in Practice and Theory," *Public Administration Review* 44 (Special Issue, March 1984): 120–25; John J. Kirlin, "Policy Formulation," in *Making and Managing Policy: Formulation, Analysis, Evaluation,* ed. G. Ronald Gilbert (New York: Dekker, 1984), 13–24; David K. Hart, "The Honorable Bureaucrat Among the Philistines," *Administration and Society* 15, 1 (May 1983): 43–48; and John A. Rohr, *Ethics for Bureaucrats* (New York: Dekker, 1978). See also Max Weber, *Economy and Society,* ed. Guenther Roth and Claus Wittich (Berkeley: University of California Press, 1978), 2: 1451; Herbert Kaufman, "Fear of Bureaucracy: A Raging Pandemic," *Public Administration Review* 41, 1 (January/February 1981): 7; Waldo, *Enterprise of Public Administration,* 36–43; William G. Scott, "Barnard on the Nature of Elitist Responsibility," *Public Administration Review* 42, 3 (May/June 1982): 197–201; David K. Hart and William G. Scott, "The Philosophy of American Management," *Southern Review of Public Administration* 6, 2 (Summer 1982): 240–52; Robert B. Denhardt, "Toward a Critical Theory of Public Organization," *Public Administration Review* 41, 6 (November/December 1981): 628–35; and Douglas Yates, *Bureaucratic Democracy* (Cambridge: Harvard University Press, 1982).

44. Franklin D. Roosevelt, *The Roosevelt Reader: Selected Speeches, Messages, Press Conferences, and Letters of Franklin D. Roosevelt,* ed. B. Rauch (New York: Rinehart and Company, 1957), 62–63.

45. Ibid., 347.

46. Ibid.

47. Tocqueville, *Democracy in America,* 515.

48. Arthur A. Schlesinger, Jr., *The Coming of the New Deal* (Boston: Houghton Mifflin, 1958), 3.

49. Ibid., 515–47.

50. George A. Gallup, *The Gallup Poll, Public Opinion 1935–1971* (New York: Random House, 1972), 1: 12ff; and Warren E. Miller, Arthur H. Miller, and Edward J. Schneider, *American National Election Studies Data Sourcebook* (Cambridge: Harvard University Press, 1980), 171–90, 255–72.

51. See Lynton K. Caldwell, "Alexander Hamilton: Advocate of Executive Leadership," in *Administrative Questions and Political Answers,* ed. Claude E. Hawley and Ruth G. Weintraub (New York: D. Van Nostrand, 1966), 16–22; Morton J. Frisch, *Franklin D. Roosevelt: The Contributions of the New Deal to American Political Thought and Practice* (Boston: Twayne, 1975); Thomas H. Greer, *What Roosevelt Thought: The Social and Political Ideas of Franklin Roosevelt* (East Lansing: Michigan State University Press, 1958); Rexford G. Tugwell, *Roosevelt's Revolution: The First Year—A Personal Perspective* (New York: Macmillan, 1977); and William E. Leuchtenburg, *In the Shadow of FDR: From Harry Truman to Ronald Reagan* (Ithaca, N.Y.: Cornell University Press, 1983).

52. Hubert H. Humphrey, *The Political Philosophy of the New Deal* (Baton Rouge: Louisiana State University Press, 1970), x.

53. Weber, *Economy and Society,* 2: 1451; Kaufman, "Fear of Bureaucracy," 7; Waldo, *Enterprise of Public Administration,* 36–43; Scott, "Barnard on the Nature of Elitist Responsibility," 197–201; Hart and Scott, "Philosophy of American Management," 240–52; Denhardt, "Toward a Critical Theory of Public Organization," 628–35; Wildavsky, *Speaking Truth to Power,* 109–41; and Yates, *Bureaucratic Democracy.*

54. Alexis de Tocqueville, *Journey to America,* ed. J. P. Mayer (Garden City, N.Y.: Anchor Books, 1971), 38–39.

55. Schlesinger, *Coming of the New Deal,* 72.

56. Ibid., 87–176, and Hugh S. Johnson, *The Blue Eagle from Egg to Earth* (Garden City, N.Y.: Doubleday, Doran and Company, 1935).

57. Schlesinger, *Coming of the New Deal,* 175.

58. Ibid., 174.

59. Ibid., 308–9.

60. Robert Dahl and Charles Lindblom, *Politics, Economics, and Welfare* (New York: Harper and Row, 1953), 3–54.

61. Marc Plattner, "The Welfare State vs. the Redistributive State," *Public Interest* 55 (Spring 1979): 28–48.

62. Schlesinger, *Coming of the New Deal,* 262–81. These sentiments are strikingly similar to Republican ones currently expressed in Gillespie and Schellhas, eds., *Contract with America,* 65–78.

63. Schlesinger, *Coming of the New Deal,* 298.
64. Virtually all commentators note FDR's "a-theoretical" approach; see, for example, Paul K. Conklin, *FDR and the Origins of the Welfare State* (New York: Thomas Y. Crowell, 1967); Howard Zinn, ed., *New Deal Thought* (Indianapolis: Bobbs-Merrill, 1966); A. J. Wann, *The President as Chief Administrator: A Study of Franklin D. Roosevelt* (Washington, D.C.: Public Affairs Press, 1968); and James MacGregor Burns, *Roosevelt: The Lion and the Fox* (New York: Harcourt, Brace and World, 1956).
65. Storing, "American Statesmanship," 98. See also Dahl and Lindblom, *Politics, Economics, and Welfare,* 511–26.

CHAPTER 7. ADMINISTRATIVE ETHICS
AND FOUNDING THOUGHT

1. Aristotle, *Politics,* ed. and trans. Ernest Barker (New York: Oxford University Press, 1946), 1253a15ff.
2. See Martin Diamond's development of this argument in his "Ethics and Politics: The American Way," in *The Moral Foundations of the American Republic,* ed. Robert H. Horwitz, 2d ed. (Charlottesville: University Press of Virginia, 1979), esp. 40–44.
3. See ibid., 40.
4. Gordon Wood, "Interests and Disinterestedness in the Making of the Constitution," in *Beyond Confederation: Origins of the Constitution and American National Identity,* ed. Richard Beeman, Stephen Botein, and Edward C. Carter II (Chapel Hill: University of North Carolina Press, 1987), 82.
5. *Federalist Papers,* 350.
6. Ralph Lerner, "The Constitution of the Thinking Revolutionary," in Beeman et al., eds., *Beyond Confederation,* 59.
7. John Rohr, quoted in "The Constitution and Public Service," in *The Constitution and the Administration of Government,* ed. Gary C. Bryner (Washington, D.C.: NAPA, 1988), 58.
8. *Federalist Papers,* 435.
9. Jeremy Rabkin, "Bureaucratic Idealism and Executive Power: A Perspective on the Federalists' View of Public Administration," in *Saving the Revolution,* ed. Charles Kesler (New York: Free Press, 1987), 196–98.
10. Robert D. Miewald, "The Origins of Wilson's Thought—The German Tradition and the Organic State," in *Politics and Administration,* ed. Jack Rabin & James Bowman (New York: Dekker, 1984), 27–28.
11. Dwight Waldo, *The Administrative State* (New York: Ronald Press, 1948), 97–100.

12. Robert Goldwin, "Of Men and Angels: The Search for Morality in the Constitution," in Horwitz, ed., *Moral Foundations*, 9–12.

13. Thomas Jefferson, *Notes on the State of Virginia,* ed. William Peden (New York: W. W. Norton, 1972), 146–49.

14. Gordon Wood, *The Creation of the American Republic, 1776–1787* (New York: Norton, 1969), 508.

15. Ibid., 475.

16. James MacGregor Burns, *The Vineyard of Liberty* (New York: Vintage Books, 1983), 62.

17. Wood, "Interests and Disinterestedness," 92.

18. Ibid., 84.

19. Ibid., 109.

20. Ralph Clarke Chandler, "The Problem of Moral Reasoning in American Public Administration: The Case for a Code of Ethics," *Public Administration Review* 43 (January/February 1983): 37.

21. David K. Hart, "The Honorable Bureaucrat Among the Philistines," *Administration and Society* 15, 1 (May 1983): 44.

22. John Rohr, "Civil Servants and Second-Class Citizens," *Public Administration Review* 44 (March 1984): 139–40.

23. David K. Hart, "Public Administration, the Thoughtless Functionary, and 'Feelinglessness,'" in *The Revitalization of the Public Service,* ed. Robert B. Denhardt and Edward T. Jennings, Jr. (Columbia: University of Missouri–Columbia Extension Publications, 1987), 78 (emphasis added).

24. For example, see H. G. Frederickson and David K. Hart, "The Public Service and the Patriotism of Benevolence," *Public Administration Review* 45 (September/October 1985): 547–53.

25. Morton White, *Philosophy, the Federalist, and the Constitution* (New York: Oxford University Press, 1987), 122.

26. Lerner, "Constitution of the Thinking Revolutionary," 65.

27. Wood, "Interests and Disinterestedness," 82.

28. Cecilia Kenyon, "Men of Little Faith: The Anti-Federalists on the Nature of Representative Government," in *The Formation and Ratification of the Constitution: Major Historical Interpretations,* ed. Kermit L. Hall (New York: Garland, 1987), 383.

29. White, *Philosophy,* 202–3.

30. Lynton Caldwell, *The Administrative Theories of Hamilton and Jefferson* (Chicago: University of Chicago Press. 1944), 13.

31. Waldo, *Administrative State,* 100.

32. *Federalist Papers,* 322 (emphasis added).

33. Chandler, "The Problem of Moral Reasoning," 37.

34. Alexis de Tocqueville, *Democracy in America,* ed. J. P. Mayer (Garden City, N.Y.: Anchor Books, 1969), 525–28.

35. Ibid., 525.

36. Slightly different versions of this argument as they pertain to some contemporary political battles are provided by Michael Kazin, *The Populist Persuasion: An American History* (New York: Basic Books, 1994), and Christopher Lasch, *The Revolt of the Elites: And the Betrayal of Democracy* (New York: W. W. Norton, 1995).

37. Diamond, "Ethics and Politics," 62.

38. Ibid., 67.

39. White, *Philosophy,* 98–99.

40. Woodrow Wilson, "The Study of Administration," in *Public Administration, Politics and the People,* ed. Dean Yarwood (White Plains, N.Y.: Longman, 1987), 20–30.

41. John Rohr, *Ethics for Bureaucrats,* 2d ed. (New York: Dekker, 1989), 30–34.

42. Wilson, "Study of Administration," 28.

CHAPTER 8. EPILOGUE

1. K. L. Billingsley, "Off the Charts: The NEA Does Charter Schools," *Report Card* 2 (May/June 1996): 1, 13–14.

2. Arthur A. Schlesinger, Jr., *The Coming of the New Deal* (Boston: Houghton Mifflin, 1958), 72.

3. William G. Scott, "Barnard on the Nature of Elitist Responsibility," *Public Administration Review* 42, 3 (May/June 1982): 197–201, and Frederick C. Thayer, *An End to Hierarchy and Competition: Administration in the Post-Affluent World,* 2d ed. (New York: Franklin Watts, 1981).

4. Alexis de Tocqueville, *Journey to America,* ed. J. P. Mayer (Garden City, N.Y.: Anchor Books, 1971), 38–39.

5. Scott, "Barnard on the Nature of Elitist Responsibility," 197–201.

6. Herbert Storing, "American Statesmanship: Old and New," in *Bureaucrats, Policy Analysts, Statesmen: Who Leads?* ed. Robert Goldwin (Washington, D.C.: American Enterprise Institute, 1980), 92–93.

7. Charles T. Goodsell, *The Case for Bureaucracy: A Public Administration Polemic* (Chatham, N.J.: Chatham House Publishers, 1983), 11.

Bibliography

Adams, Bruce. "The Frustrations of Government Service." *Public Administration Review* 44 (January/February 1984): 5–13.

Almond, Gabriel A., and Sidney Verba. *The Civic Culture.* Princeton: Princeton University Press, 1963.

Appleby, Paul H. *Big Democracy.* New York: Alfred A. Knopf, 1949.

———. "Toward Better Public Administration." *Public Administration Review* 7, no. 2 (1947): 93–99.

Aristophanes. *Lysistrata.* Edited by Jeffrey Henderson. New York: Oxford University Press, 1987.

Aristotle. *The Nicomachean Ethics.* Translated by H. Rackham. Cambridge: Harvard University Press, 1934.

———. *The Politics of Aristotle.* Edited and translated by Ernest Barker. New York: Oxford University Press, 1946.

Axtell, James L., ed. *The Educational Writings of John Locke.* Cambridge: Cambridge University Press, 1968.

Bailey, Stephen K. "Ethics and the Public Service." In *Public Administration and Democracy.* Edited by Roscoe C. Martin, 283–98. Syracuse, N.Y.: Syracuse University Press, 1965.

———. "Ethics and the Public Service." In *Public Administration: Concepts and Cases.* Edited by Richard J. Stillman II, 480–89. 3d ed. Boston: Houghton Mifflin, 1984.

Beeman, Richard, Stephen Botein, and Edward C. Carter II. *Beyond Confederation: Origins of the Constitution and American National Identity.* Chapel Hill: University of North Carolina Press, 1987.

Bendix, Reinhard. *Max Weber: An Intellectual Portrait*. Garden City, N.Y.: Anchor Books, Doubleday and Company, 1962.

Billingsley, K. L. "Off the Charts: The NEA Does Charter Schools." *Report Card* 2 (May/June 1996): 1, 13–14.

Boswell, James. *Boswell's Life of Johnson*. Vol. 2. London: Oxford University Press, 1934.

Boyd, Julian P., et al., eds. *The Papers of Thomas Jefferson*. 26 vols. Princeton: Princeton University Press, 1950.

Burnham, William. "The Constitution, Capitalism, and the Need for Rationalized Regulation." In *How Capitalistic Is the Constitution?* Edited by Robert Goldwin and W. Schambra, 75–105. Washington, D.C.: American Enterprise Institute, 1982.

Burns, James MacGregor. *Roosevelt: The Lion and the Fox*. New York: Harcourt, Brace and World, 1956.

———. *The Vineyard of Liberty*. New York: Vintage Books, 1983.

Caiden, Gerald E. "In Search of an Apolitical Science of American Public Administration." In *Politics and Administration: Woodrow Wilson and American Public Administration*. Edited by Jack S. Rabin and James S. Bowman, 51–76. New York: Dekker, 1984.

Caldwell, Lynton K. *The Administrative Theories of Hamilton and Jefferson*. Chicago: University of Chicago Press, 1944.

———. "Alexander Hamilton: Advocate of Executive Leadership." *Public Administration Review* 4 (1944): 113–26.

———. "Alexander Hamilton: Advocate of Executive Leadership." In *Administrative Questions and Political Answers*. Edited by Claude E. Hawley and Ruth G. Weintraub, 16–22. New York: D. Van Nostrand Company, 1966.

———. "Thomas Jefferson and Public Administration." *Public Administration Review* 3 (1943): 240–53.

Cappon, Lester J., ed. *The Adams-Jefferson Letters*. 2 vols. Chapel Hill: University of North Carolina Press, 1959.

Chandler, Ralph Clark. "The Problem of Moral Reasoning in American Public Administration: The Case for a Code of Ethics." *Public Administration Review* 43 (January/February 1983): 32–39.

Conant, James B., ed. *Thomas Jefferson and the Development of American Public Education*. Berkeley: University of California Press, 1962.

Conklin, Paul K. *FDR and the Origins of the Welfare State*. New York: Thomas Y. Crowell Company, 1967.

Cooper, Phillip J. *Public Law and Public Administration*. Palo Alto, Calif.: Mayfield Publishing Company, 1983.

———. "The Wilsonian Dichotomy in Administrative Law." In *Politics and Administration: Woodrow Wilson and American Public Adminis-*

tration. Edited by Jack Rabin and James Bowman, 79–94. New York: Dekker, 1984.

Cropsey, Joseph. *Political Philosophy and the Issues of Politics*. Chicago: University of Chicago Press, 1980.

Dahl, Robert, and Charles Lindblom. *Politics, Economics, and Welfare*. New York: Harper and Row, 1953.

Davis, Kenneth Culp. *Discretionary Justice: A Preliminary Inquiry*. Baton Rouge: Louisiana State University Press, 1969.

Denhardt, Robert B. "Toward a Critical Theory of Public Organization." *Public Administration Review* 41, no. 6 (November/December 1981): 628–35.

Diamond, Martin. "The American Idea of Man: The View from the Founding." In *Critical Choices for Americans*. Edited by Irving Kristol and Paul Weaver, 2:1–23. Lexington, Mass.: Lexington Books, 1975.

———. "Ethics and Politics: The American Way." In *The Moral Foundations of the American Republic*. Edited by Robert H. Horwitz, 39–72. 2d ed. Charlottesville: University of Virginia Press, 1979.

———. "The Federalist." In *American Political Thought: The Philosophic Dimension of American Statesmanship*. Edited by Morton J. Frisch and Richard G. Stevens, 51–70. 2d ed. Itasca, Ill.: F. E. Peacock, 1983.

Doig, Jameson W. " 'If I See a Murderous Fellow Sharpening a Knife Cleverly . . .': The Wilsonian Dichotomy and the Public Authority Tradition." *Public Administration Review* 43 (July/August 1983): 292–304.

Edelman, Murray. *Political Language: Words That Succeed and Policies That Fail*. New York: Academic Press, 1977.

Elshtain, Jean Bethke. *Democracy on Trial*. New York: Basic Books, 1995.

Farrand, Max, ed. *The Records of the Federal Convention of 1787*. New Haven: Yale University Press, 1937.

Finer, Herman. "Democratic Responsibility in Democratic Government." *Public Administration Review* 1, no. 4 (1941): 335–50.

Fleishman, Joel L. "Self-Interest and Political Integrity." In *Public Duties: The Moral Obligations of Government Officials*. Edited by Joel L. Fleishman, Lance Liebman, and Mark H. Moore, 52–92. Cambridge: Harvard University Press, 1981.

Fleishman, Joel L., Lance Liebman, and Mark H. Moore, eds. *Public Duties: The Moral Obligations of Government Officials*. Cambridge: Harvard University Press, 1981.

Fleming, Arthur S. "The Civil Servant in a Period of Transition." *Public Administration Review* 13, no. 2 (1953): 73–79.

Frederickson, H. George. *New Public Administration*. University: University of Alabama Press, 1980.

———. "The Recovery of Civism in Public Administration." *Public Administration Review* 42, no. 6 (November/December 1982): 501–8.

Frederickson, H. George, and David K. Hart. "The Public Service and the Patriotism of Benevolence." *Public Administration Review* 45 (September/October 1985): 547–53.

Frederickson, H. George, and Ralph C. Chandler, eds. "Citizenship and Public Administration." *Public Administration Review* 45 (Special Issue 1984).

Frieden, Bernard J. "The New Regulation Comes to Suburbia." *Public Interest* 55 (Spring 1979): 15–27.

Friedman, Milton. *Capitalism and Freedom*. Chicago: University of Chicago Press, 1962.

Friedman, Milton, and Rose Friedman. *Free to Choose: A Personal Statement*. New York: Harcourt Brace Jovanovich, 1980.

———. *Tyranny of the Status Quo*. San Diego, Calif.: Harcourt Brace Javanovich, 1984.

Friedrich, Carl J. *An Introduction to Political Theory*. New York: Harper and Row, 1967.

Frisch, Morton J. *Franklin D. Roosevelt: The Contributions of the New Deal to American Political Thought and Practice*. Boston: Twayne, 1975.

Frisch, Morton J., and Richard G. Stevens, eds. *American Political Thought: The Philosophic Dimension of American Statesmanship*. 2d ed. Itasca, Ill.: F. E. Peacock, 1983.

Gallup, George A. *The Gallup Poll, Public Opinion 1935–1971*. New York: Random House, 1972.

Gawthrop, Louis C. "Civas, Civitas, and Civilitas: A New Focus for the Year 2000." *Public Administration Review* 44 (March/April 1984): 101–7.

Gilder, George. *Wealth and Poverty*. New York: Basic Books, 1981.

Gillespie, Ed, and Bob Schellhas, eds. *Contract with America*. New York: Times Books, 1995.

Glassberg, Andrew D. "The Urban Fiscal Crisis Becomes Routine." *Public Administration Review* 41 (Special Issue 1981): 165–72.

Goldwin, Robert A. "John Locke." In *History of Political Philosophy*. Edited by Leo Strauss and Joseph Cropsey, 451–86. 2d ed. Chicago: Rand McNally College Publishing Company, 1972.

———. "Of Men and Angels: A Search for Morality in the Constitution." In *The Moral Foundations of the American Republic*. Edited by Robert Horwitz, 1–18. 2d ed. Charlottesville: University Press of Virginia, 1979.

Goldwin, Robert A., ed. *Bureaucrats, Policy Analysts, Statesmen: Who Leads?* Washington, D.C.: American Enterprise Institute, 1980.

Goldwin, Robert A., and William A. Schambra, eds. *How Capitalistic Is the Constitution?* Washington, D.C.: American Enterprise Institute, 1982.

_____. *How Democratic Is the Constitution?* Washington, D.C.: American Enterprise Institute, 1980.

Goodsell, Charles T. *The Case for Bureaucracy: A Public Administration Polemic.* Chatham, N.J.: Chatham House Publishers, 1983.

_____. "The Grace Commission: Seeking Efficiency for the Whole People?" *Public Administration Review* 44 (May/June 1984): 196–204.

Greer, Thomas H. *What Roosevelt Thought: The Social and Political Ideas of Franklin Roosevelt.* East Lansing: Michigan State University Press, 1958.

Hall, Kermit L., ed. *The Formation and Ratification of the Constitution: Major Historical Interpretations.* New York: Garland Publishing, 1987.

Hamilton, Alexander, James Madison, and John Jay. *The Federalist Papers.* Introduction by Clinton Rossiter. New York: New American Library, 1961.

Harmon, Michael M. "Administrative Policy Formation and the Public Interest." *Public Administration Review* 24 (September/October 1969): 483–91.

Hart, David K. "The Honorable Bureaucrat Among the Philistines." *Administration and Society* 15, no. 1 (May 1983): 43–48.

_____. "Public Administration, the Thoughtless Functionary, and 'Feelinglessness.' " In *The Revitalization of the Public Service.* Edited by Robert B. Denhardt and Edward T. Jennings, Jr., 77–97. Columbia: University of Missouri–Columbia Extension Publications, 1987.

_____. "The Virtuous Citizen, the Honorable Bureaucrat, and 'Public' Administration." *Public Administration Review* 44 (March 1984): 111–20.

Hart, David K., and William G. Scott. "The Philosophy of American Management." *Southern Review of Public Administration* 6, no. 2 (1982): 240–52.

Hawley, Claude E., and Ruth G. Weintraub, eds. *Administrative Questions and Political Answers.* New York: D. Van Nostrand Company, 1966.

Hayek, Friedrich A. *Individualism and Economic Order.* Chicago: University of Chicago Press, 1949.

_____. *The Road to Serfdom.* Chicago: University of Chicago Press, 1944.

Hofstadter, Richard. "The Founding Fathers: An Age of Realism." In *The Moral Foundations of the American Republic.* Edited by Robert H.

Horwitz, 73–85. 2d ed. Charlottesville: University Press of Virginia, 1979.

Horwitz, Robert H. "John Locke and the Preservation of Liberty: A Perennial Problem of Civic Education." In *The Moral Foundations of the American Republic*. Edited by Robert H. Horwitz, 129–56. 2d ed. Charlottesville: University Press of Virginia, 1979.

Horwitz, Robert H., ed. *The Moral Foundations of the American Republic*. 2d ed. Charlottesville: University Press of Virginia, 1979.

Humphrey, Hubert H. *The Political Philosophy of the New Deal*. Baton Rouge: Louisiana State University Press, 1970.

Jefferson, Thomas. *Notes on the State of Virginia*. Edited by William Peden. New York: W. W. Norton, 1972.

———. *The Papers of Thomas Jefferson*. 26 vols. Edited by Julian P. Boyd et al. Princeton: Princeton University Press, 1950.

Johnson, Hugh S. *The Blue Eagle from Egg to Earth*. Garden City, N.Y.: Doubleday, Doran and Company, 1935.

Jouvenel, Bertrand de. *The Ethics of Redistribution*. Cambridge: Cambridge University Press, 1952.

Karl, Barry D. *Executive Reorganization and Reform in the New Deal*. Cambridge: Harvard University Press, 1963.

Kaufman, Herbert. "Fear of Bureaucracy: A Raging Pandemic." *Public Administration Review* 41, no. 1 (January/February 1981): 1–9.

Kazin, Michael. *The Populist Persuasion: An American History*. New York: Basic Books, 1995.

Kenyon, Cecilia. "Men of Little Faith: The Anti-Federalists on the Nature of Representative Government." In *The Formation and Ratification of the Constitution: Major Historical Interpretations*. Edited by Kermit L. Hall, 348–88. New York: Garland, 1987.

Kesler, Charles R., ed. *Saving the Revolution: The Federalist Papers and the American Founding*. New York: Free Press, 1987.

Kirlin, John J. "Policy Formulation." In *Making and Managing Policy: Formulation, Analysis, Evaluation*. Edited by G. Ronald Gilbert, 13–24. New York: Dekker, 1984.

Kristol, Irving. " 'When Virtue Loses All Her Loveliness'—Some Reflections on Capitalism and 'The Free Society.' " *Public Interest* 21 (Fall 1970): 3–15.

Kristol, Irving, and Paul Weaver, eds. *Critical Choices for Americans*. Lexington, Mass.: Lexington Books, 1975.

Laffer, Arthur B., and Jan P. Seymour. *The Economics of the Tax Revolt*. New York: Harcourt Brace Jovanovich, 1979.

Landis, James M. *The Administrative Process*. Westport, Conn.: Greenwood Press, 1974.

Lasch, Christopher. *The Revolt of the Elites and the Betrayal of Democracy.* New York: W. W. Norton, 1995.

Lerner, Ralph. "The Constitution of the Thinking Revolutionary." In *Beyond Confederation: Origins of the Constitution and American National Identity.* Edited by Richard Beeman, Stephen Botein, and Edward C. Carter II, 38–68. Chapel Hill: University of North Carolina Press, 1987.

Leuchtenburg, William E. *In the Shadow of FDR: From Harry Truman to Ronald Reagan.* Ithaca, N.Y.: Cornell University Press, 1983.

Levine, Charles H. "Organizational Decline and Cutback Management." *Public Administration Review* 38 (July/August 1978): 316–25.

Levitan, David M. "The Neutrality of the Public Service." *Public Administration Review* 2, no. 4 (1942): 317–23.

Levy, Michael B. *Political Thought in America: An Anthology.* Homewood, Ill.: Dorsey Press, 1982.

Lincoln, Abraham. "Address Before the Young Men's Lyceum of Springfield, Illinois." In *The Collected Works of Abraham Lincoln.* Edited by Roy P. Basler, 1: 108–15. New Brunswick, N.J.: Rutgers University Press, 1953.

Lindblom, Charles E. *Politics and Markets.* New York: Basic Books, 1977.

Locke, John. *Some Thoughts Concerning Education.* Edited by F. W. Garforth. Woodbury, N.Y.: Barron's Educational Series, 1964.

_____. *Two Treatises of Government.* Edited by Thomas I. Cooke. New York: Hafner, 1947.

Lowi, Theodore. *The End of Liberalism.* 2d ed. New York: W. W. Norton, 1979.

McDonald, Forrest. "The Constitution and Hamiltonian Capitalism." In *How Capitalistic Is the Constitution?* Edited by Robert A Goldwin and William A. Schambra, 49–74. Washington, D.C.: American Enterprise Institute, 1982.

_____. *Novus Ordo Seclorum: The Intellectual Origins of the Constitution.* Lawrence: University Press of Kansas, 1985.

McWilliams, Wilson Carey. "Democracy and the Citizen: Community, Dignity, and the Crisis of Contemporary Politics in America." In *How Democratic Is the Constitution?* Edited by Robert A. Goldwin and William A. Schambra, 79–101. Washington, D.C.: American Enterprise Institute, 1980.

_____. "On Equality as the Moral Foundation for Community." In *The Moral Foundations of the American Republic.* Edited by Robert Horwitz, 183–213. 2d ed. Charlottesville: University of Virginia Press, 1979.

Martin, D. W. "The Fading Legacy of Woodrow Wilson." *Public Administration Review* 48 (March/April 1988): 631–36.

Martin, Roscoe C., ed. *Public Administration and Democracy.* Syracuse, N.Y.: Syracuse University Press, 1965.

Mathews, David. "The Public in Practice and Theory." *Public Administration Review* 44 (Special Issue, March 1984): 120–25.

Miewald, Robert D. "The Origins of Wilson's Thought—The German Tradition and the Organic State." In *Politics and Administration: Woodrow Wilson and American Public Administration.* Edited by Jack Rabin and James Bowman, 17–30. New York: Dekker, 1984.

Miller, John Chester. *The Wolf by the Ears: Thomas Jefferson and Slavery.* New York: Free Press, 1977.

Miller, Warren E., Arthur H. Miller, and Edward J. Schneider. *American National Election Studies Data Sourcebook.* Cambridge: Harvard University Press, 1980.

Mosher, Frederick C. "The Professional State." In *Public Administration, Politics, and the People: Selected Readings for Managers, Employees, and Citizens.* Edited by Dean L. Yarwood, 187–98. White Plains, N.Y.: Longman, 1987.

———. "Professions in Public Service." *Public Administration Review* 38 (March/April 1978): 144–50.

Moulds, Henry. "Private Property in John Locke's State of Nature." *American Journal of Economics and Sociology* 23 (1964): 179–88.

NASPAA Commission on Peer Review and Accreditation. *Self-Study Report Instructions.* Washington, D.C., July 1994.

Novak, Michael. *The American Vision: An Essay on the Future of Democratic Capitalism.* Washington, D.C.: American Enterprise Institute, 1978.

Opinion News 9 (1947).

Osborne, David, and Ted Gabler. *Reinventing Government: How the Entrepreneurial Spirit Is Transforming the Public Sector from Schoolhouse to Statehouse, City Hall to the Pentagon.* New York: Addison-Wesley Publishing Company, 1992.

Ostrom, Vincent. *The Intellectual Crisis in American Public Administration.* University: University of Alabama Press, 1974.

O'Toole, Laurence J., Jr. "American Public Administration and the Idea of Reform." *Administration and Society* 16 (1984): 141–66.

Pangle, Lorraine Smith, and Thomas L. Pangle. *The Learning of Liberty: The Educational Ideas of the American Founders.* Lawrence: University Press of Kansas, 1993.

Parsons, John E., Jr. "Locke's Doctrine of Property." *Social Research* 36 (1969): 389–411.

Plato. *The Republic*. Translated by Allan Bloom. New York: Basic Books, 1968.

Plattner, Marc. "The Welfare State vs. the Redistributive State." *Public Interest* 55 (Spring 1979): 28–48.

Plutarch. "Lycurgus." In *The Lives of the Noble Grecians and Romans.* Translated by John Dryden, 49–74. New York: Modern Library, 1932.

_____. "Lycurgus." In *The Quest for Justice: Readings in Political Ethics.* Edited by Leslie G. Rubin and Charles T. Rubin, 11–33. Needham Heights, Mass.: Ginn Press, 1987.

Rabin, Jack, and James Bowman, eds. *Politics and Administration: Woodrow Wilson and American Public Administration.* New York: Dekker, 1984.

Rabkin, Jeremy. "Bureaucratic Idealism and Executive Power: A Perspective on *The Federalist*'s View of Public Administration." In *Saving the Revolution: The Federalist Papers and the American Founding.* Edited by Charles R. Kesler, 185–202. New York: Free Press, 1987.

Redford, Emmette S. *Administration of National Economic Control.* New York: Macmillan, 1972.

_____. *Democracy in the Administrative State.* New York: Oxford University Press, 1969.

Richardson, William D. "Thomas Jefferson and Race: The Declaration and *Notes on the State of Virginia.*" *Polity* 16 (Spring 1984): 447–66.

Rohr, John A. "Civil Servants and Second-Class Citizens." *Public Administration Review* 44 (March 1984): 135–40.

_____. Quoted in "The Constitution and Public Service." In *The Constitution and the Administration of Government.* Edited by Gary C. Bryner. Washington, D.C.: NAPA, 1988.

_____. *Ethics for Bureaucrats.* New York: Dekker, 1978.

_____. "The Study of Ethics in the P.A. Curriculum." *Public Administration Review* 36 (July/August 1976): 398–406.

_____. *To Run a Constitution: The Legitimacy of the Administrative State.* Lawrence: University of Kansas Press, 1986.

Roosevelt, Franklin D. *The Roosevelt Reader: Selected Speeches, Messages, Press Conferences, and Letters of Franklin D. Roosevelt.* Edited by B. Rauch. New York: Rinehart and Company, 1957.

Rossum, Ralph A., and Gary L. McDowell, eds. *The American Founding: Politics, Statesmanship, and the Constitution.* Port Washington, N.Y.: Kennikat Press, 1981.

Rubin, Leslie G., and Charles T. Rubin, eds. *The Quest for Justice: Readings in Political Ethics.* Needham Heights, Mass.: Ginn Press, 1987.

Schambra, William A. "Martin Diamond's Doctrine of the American Regime." *Publius* 8 (1978): 213–18.

Schaub, Diana. "Review of *The Learning of Liberty.*" *Academic Questions* 8 (Spring 1995): 93–98.

Schiesl, Martin J. *The Politics of Efficiency: Municipal Administration and Reform in America.* Berkeley: University of California Press, 1977.

Schlesinger, Arthur M. *The Age of Roosevelt: The Crisis of the Old Order, 1919–1933.* Boston: Houghton Mifflin, 1957.

———. *The Age of Roosevelt: The Politics of Upheaval.* Boston: Houghton Mifflin, 1960.

———. *The Coming of the New Deal.* Boston: Houghton Mifflin, 1958.

Scott, William G. "Barnard on the Nature of Elitist Responsibility." *Public Administration Review* 42, no. 3 (May/June 1982): 197–201.

Smith, Adam. *The Theory of Moral Sentiments.* Edited by D. D. Raphael and A. L. Macfie. Indianapolis: Liberty Classics, 1976.

———. *The Wealth of Nations.* Edited by Edwin Cannan. New York: G. P. Putnam's Sons, 1904.

Somit, Albert, and Joseph Tannenhause. *The Development of American Political Science: From Burgess to Behavioralism.* New York: Irvington Publishers, 1982.

Sowell, Thomas. *Markets and Minorities.* New York: Basic Books, 1981.

Spicer, Michael. *The Founders, the Constitution, and Public Administration: A Conflict in World Views.* Washington, D.C.: Georgetown University Press, 1995.

Stillman, Richard J., II. *Public Administration: Concepts and Cases.* 3d ed. Boston: Houghton Mifflin, 1984.

Storing, Herbert J. "American Statesmanship: Old and New." In *Bureaucrats, Policy Analysts, Statesmen: Who Leads?* Edited by Robert A. Goldwin, 88–113. Washington, D.C.: American Enterprise Institute, 1980.

———. "Leonard D. White and the Study of Public Administration." *Public Administration Review* 25 (March 1965): 38–51.

———. *What the Anti-Federalists Were For: The Political Thought of the Opponents of the Constitution.* Chicago: University of Chicago Press, 1981.

Strauss, Leo. *On Tyranny.* Glencoe, Ill.: Free Press of Glencoe, 1963.

———. "Plato." In *History of Political Philosophy.* Edited by Leo Strauss and Joseph Cropsey, 7–63. 2d ed. Chicago: Rand McNally College Publishing Company, 1972.

Strauss, Leo, and Joseph Cropsey, eds. *History of Political Philosophy.* 2d ed. Chicago: Rand McNally College Publishing Company, 1971.

Taylor, Sir Henry. *The Statesman.* Edited by David Lewis Schaefer and Roberta Rubel Schaefer. Westport, Conn.: Praeger Publishers, 1992.

Thayer, Frederick C. *An End to Hierarchy and Competition: Administration in the Post-Affluent World.* 2d ed. New York: Franklin Watts, 1981.

To Serve with Honor: Report of the President's Commission on Federal Ethics Law Reform. Petersburg, Va.: Unicor Print Plant, 1989.

Tocqueville, Alexis de. *Democracy in America.* Edited by J. P. Mayer. Garden City, N.Y.: Anchor Books, 1969.

———. *Journey to America.* Edited by J. P. Mayer. Garden City, N.Y.: Anchor Books, 1971.

Tolchin, Susan J., and Martin Tolchin. *Dismantling America: The Rush to Deregulate.* Boston: Houghton Mifflin, 1983.

Tucker, David. "The Political Thought of Thomas Jefferson's *Notes on the State of Virginia.*" In *The American Founding: Politics, Statesmanship, and the Constitution.* Edited by Ralph A. Rossum and Gary L. McDowell, 108–21. Port Washington, N.Y.: Kennikat Press, 1981.

Tugwell, Rexford G. *Roosevelt's Revolution: The First Year—A Personal Perspective.* New York: Macmillan, 1977.

U.S. Department of Commerce. Bureau of the Census. *Historical Statistics of the United States: Colonial Times to 1970.* Washington, D.C.: U.S. Government Printing Office, 1975.

Van Riper, Paul P. "The American Administrative State: Wilson and the Founders—An Unorthodox View." *Public Administration Review* 43 (November/December 1983): 477–90.

———. *History of the United States Civil Service.* Chicago: Row, Peterson, 1958.

Waldo, Dwight. *The Administrative State.* New York: Ronald Press, 1948.

———. *The Enterprise of Public Administration.* Novato, Calif.: Chandler and Sharp Publishers, 1980.

———. "The Perdurability of the Politics-Administration Dichotomy: Woodrow Wilson and the Identity Crisis in Public Administration." In *Politics and Administration: Woodrow Wilson and American Public Administration.* Edited by Jack S. Rabin and James S. Bowman, 219–33. New York: Dekker, 1984.

Wann, A. J. *The President as Chief Administrator: A Study of Franklin D. Roosevelt.* Washington, D.C.: Public Affairs Press, 1968.

Weber, Max. *Economy and Society.* Edited by Guenther Roth and Claus Wittich. 2 vols. Berkeley: University of California Press, 1978.

White, Morton. *Philosophy, the Federalist, and the Constitution.* New York: Oxford University Press, 1987.

Wildavsky, Aaron. *Speaking Truth to Power: The Art and Craft of Policy Analysis.* Boston: Little, Brown and Company, 1979.

Wilson, James Q., ed. *The Politics of Regulation.* New York: Basic Books, 1980.

Wilson, Woodrow. "The Study of Administration." In *The Administrative Process and Democratic Theory.* Edited by Louis C. Gawthrop, 77–85. Boston: Houghton Mifflin, 1970.

_____. "The Study of Administration." In *Public Administration, Politics, and the People: Selected Readings for Managers, Employees, and Citizens.* Edited by Dean L. Yarwood, 20–30. White Plains, N.Y.: Longman, 1987.

Wood, Gordon. *The Creation of the American Republic, 1776–1787.* New York: Norton, 1969.

_____. "Interests and Disinterestedness in the Making of the Constitution." In *Beyond Confederation: Origins of the Constitution and American National Identity.* Edited by Richard Beeman, Stephen Botein, and Edward C. Carter II, 69–109. Chapel Hill: University of North Carolina Press, 1987.

Yarwood, Dean L., ed. *Public Administration, Politics, and the People: Selected Readings for Managers, Employees, and Citizens.* White Plains, N.Y.: Longman, 1987.

Yates, Douglas. *Bureaucratic Democracy.* Cambridge: Harvard University Press, 1982.

Young, A. "Conservatives, the Constitution, and the 'Spirit of Accommodation.'" In *How Capitalistic Is the Constitution?* Edited by Robert Goldwin and W. Schambra, 117–47. Washington, D.C.: American Enterprise Institute, 1982.

Zetterbaum, Marvin. *Tocqueville and the Problem of Democracy.* Stanford, Calif.: Stanford University Press, 1967.

Zinn, Howard, ed. *New Deal Thought.* Indianapolis: Bobbs-Merrill, 1966.

Index